ANIMAL
BABIES

ANIMAL BABIES

A Habitat-by-Habitat Guide to How Wild Animals Grow

STEVE PARKER

RODALE PRESS, EMMAUS, PENNSYLVANIA

Our Mission
We publish books that empower people's lives.

RODALE BOOKS

A QUARTO BOOK

Copyright © 1994 Quarto, Inc.

This book was designed and produced by
Quarto, Inc.
The Old Brewery
6 Blundell Street
London N7 9BH

Senior Editor Sally MacEachern
Copy Editor Judy Maxwell
Senior Art Editor Mark Stevens
Designer Julie Francis
Maps David Kemp
Indexer Connie Tyler
Picture Researcher Laura Bangert
Picture Research Manager Rebecca Horsewood
Art Director Moira Clinch
Publishing Director Janet Slingsby

If you have any questions or comments concerning this book, please
write to:
Rodale Press, Inc.
Book Readers' Service
33 East Minor Street
Emmaus, PA 18098

Library of Congress Cataloging-in-Publication Data

Parker, Steve.
  Animal babies / Steve Parker.
      p. cm.
  "A Quarto book" — T.p. verso.
  Includes index.
  ISBN 0–87596–595–4 hardcover
  1. Animals — Infancy. I. Title.
QL 763. P37   1993
591. 3′9 — dc 20   93–28287
                                                                      CIP

Typeset by Bookworm Typesetting, Manchester
Manufactured in Singapore by Eray Scan Pte Ltd
Printed in Singapore by Star Standard Industries (Pte) Ltd

Distributed in the book trade by St. Martin's Press

2 4 6 8 10 9 7 5 3   hardcover

CONTENTS

INTRODUCTION

Have you ever held a new baby and thrilled at a life just beginning? Did you feel the need to nurture and protect such a tiny, helpless being? Have you played with young children and enjoyed their excitement and wonder as they learn about the world around them? These feelings help us – the older, stronger, and more experienced – to protect our young when they are most vulnerable and to give them a safe, sure start in life.

For many people, these feelings are also brought on by animal babies, although to a different degree. Kittens and puppies, lambs and calves can all stimulate the same types of emotions that we feel toward babies of our own kind. These warm, protective feelings also extend to babies of wild animals. Even people who shiver at the thought of the fully grown

Right The body proportions of these bears reveal that they are not adults but young cubs. The head is large compared to the body, and the face is more rounded, with a shorter muzzle and bigger ears.

creature – be it a mouse or a mountain lion – are captivated by the sight of a small, fluffy baby, with large trusting eyes set in a rounded face and a head that is too big for its body.

Breeding and babies

This book discusses some of the reasons why we feel so strongly attracted to babies. In doing so, it reflects on the origins of our own breeding biology and behavior.

The book also explores the breeding processes found in nature. There is an astonishing variety of ways in which animals court, mate, give birth, care for their newborn, and integrate the young into the family group or adult society. The creatures in this book range from lemmings to lions, koalas to kangaroos, penguins to pelicans, and water voles to whales.

A product of evolution

Mothers of some kinds, or species, of animals usually have just one baby, while mothers of other species have ten. Babies of some species are born hairless and helpless, with eyes and ears closed, while babies

Left Cute and cuddly, this kitten is a bundle of fluff. We feel attracted and protective of it – a spill over from our strong drive to protect our own babies.

SPECIES AND SCIENTIFIC NAMES

For each kind, or species, of animal in this book, there is a Baby Factfile that lists important information about parent and offspring. This information includes the animal species' scientific name, which is usually derived from Latin.

Common names for animals (and other living things) vary from one place to another, according to the language spoken, and the local terms and descriptions. Scientific names are useful because they are internationally agreed. They are known and understood by biologists and other life scientists in countries all around the world.

BABY FACTFILE

ANIMAL
Harp seal

SCIENTIFIC NAME
Phoca (Pagophilus) groenlandicus

DISTRIBUTION
Northern seas and coasts including the North Atlantic and Arctic Oceans from Greenland to northern Russia

SIZE OF MOTHER
Length 5-8 feet; weight 350-400 pounds

LENGTH OF PREGNANCY
49 weeks

NUMBER OF BABIES
1 pup

SIZE AT BIRTH
Weight 20 pounds

EARLY DEVELOPMENT
Feeds on rich mother's milk for 2-4 weeks, then mother leaves; pup molts fur, learns to swim and feed on fish and krill

WHEN INDEPENDENT
4 weeks

WHEN ABLE TO BREED
Females at 5 years, males at 4 years

Above *Fox pups dozing in their den are unable to defend themselves. They cannot even see, as their eyelids are still joined together.*

of other species are alert and mobile within minutes of birth.

These breeding and baby-care systems are not simply whims of nature. Modern biology explains their origins in the same way that it explains a creature's body size, tooth shape, or fur color. All are products of evolution by natural selection, sometimes referred to as the "survival of the fittest."

In order to understand why each species of animal looks after its babies in the way that it does, it helps to look at the processes of reproduction in the animal kingdom.

The process of reproduction

The diversity in the animal world is marvelous. There are soaring birds, furry mammals, teeming insects, creeping lizards, and flashing fish. There are, literally, millions of animal species on Earth.

In keeping with this wondrous diversity, there is a huge range of reproductive methods. However, they all originate from the same biological principle known as fertilization. This process involves getting

8

a female reproductive cell, or egg, from the mother to join with a male reproductive cell, or sperm, from the father.

The combined egg and sperm is so small that it can usually only be seen through a microscope. Yet it contains a complete set of instructions, or genes, to make a new, living individual. The genes are in a chemically coded form known as the substance DNA. Around these basics, animal evolution has come up with a vast array of variations.

Stages in reproduction

The whole process of reproduction may take place in several stages. These include courtship, mating, incubation or pregnancy, hatching or birth, care of the

Above Water creatures such as fish release their sperm and egg cells into the water for fertilization. This is not possible on land, since the eggs and sperm would soon dry out. Most land animals have more intimate mating methods.

Right A young skate, a fish related to both rays and sharks, feeds on the stored food reserves in the egg case left by the mother.

Below A butterfly mother will never see her baby caterpillars. She lays her eggs on plants to provide nourishment after her death.

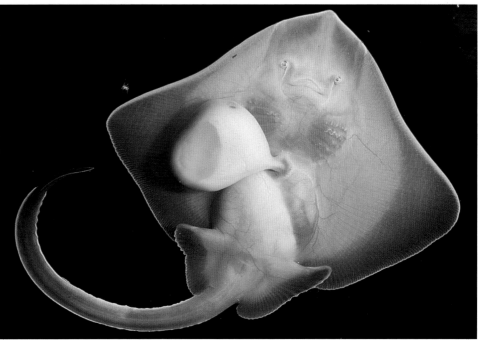

newborn, and the young growing up to become independent and mature.

Not all of these stages occur in all animal species. For example, the males and females of some sea creatures, such as starfish and sea urchins, never come together to court and mate. They simply cast their eggs and sperm into the seawater and leave fertilization to chance. In groups such as the insects and frogs, parents rarely care for their new babies. The females simply lay their eggs and leave them to their fate.

In general, reproduction has more and longer stages in more complex animals, such as birds and mammals. These are the main groups that are featured in this book.

Above *Great crested grebes present "gifts" of water weed as part of their fascinating courtship sequence.*

Courtship

Among birds and mammals, the first stage in reproduction is usually courtship. The male and female animals come together and carry out a sequence of behaviors, which varies from species to species. It can include making visual displays, adopting body poses, producing sounds, and emitting scents.

The courtship sequence helps each animal to determine that its partner is of the correct species. If an animal tries to reproduce with a member of another species, there will usually be no offspring. Even if there are, they are unlikely to survive and will never be able to breed themselves. Courtship also helps each animal to assess whether its partner is fit and healthy, and consequently a suitable mate.

Mating

After courtship, the pair mate. During mating, the male transfers his sperm to the female so fertilization can take place. This may take a few moments or much longer.

In tigers, the male and female stay together for only two or three days, yet they mate over 100 times during this period. Other species mate just once.

Some species pair for life, with the male and female remaining faithful to each other until one dies. In other species, a female mates with several

Above When toads mate, the male clasps the female securely. She lays her eggs, and at once he sheds his sperm over them.

Right Emerging from the sea to lay their eggs, powerful female loggerhead turtles may become entangled in beach furniture or crushed by beach vehicles.

males. In still others, one male may mate with several females. Almost every combination is to be found.

Egg-laying, incubation, and hatching

Most female animals lay eggs. In reptiles, such as crocodiles and turtles, the eggs have a leathery shell. In birds, the eggs usually have a harder, brittle shell.

The egg-laying period is a very risky time. Large sea turtles and crocodiles take several hours to lay an entire batch, or clutch, of eggs. Their activity or scent can easily attract predators, which slip in and steal a meal.

The fertilized egg cell develops inside the eggshell, getting energy from a food store such as the yolk. In birds, in particular, the eggs must be kept at a certain temperature for the babies inside to develop properly. Maintaining the right temperature is called incubation. Usually the parent sits on the eggs and

Left A strong predator such as this sparrowhawk can protect its brood fiercely. When the fledglings leave the nest, they are strong and capable, so the family size is relatively limited. Smaller, weaker, more defenseless birds tend to have bigger families with over a dozen chicks in some cases.

HOW MANY BABIES?

Mothers in some animal species give birth to a few babies while others have lots. The reason for this is complicated. It depends on many factors, but important ones are the animal's size and lifestyle.

Small and relatively defenseless creatures, such as mice and lemmings, are hunted by many predators. Their reproductive strategy for survival is to breed quickly and often. To keep up numbers, each mother produces several babies at a time and perhaps has several sets, or litters, in a year.

Because a female lemming or mouse is so small, she would hardly be able to walk with several well-developed babies inside her. So she gives birth to her babies while they are still small and relatively undeveloped. But they grow very fast after birth and reach maturity in only weeks or months. While they are young, their mother looks after them in a nest hidden safely away.

The offspring of larger species, such as the big cats, seals, whales, and elephants, develop within the mother for a much longer time. And they take longer to grow to maturity, too. So mothers of large species may have only one baby every several years. Their reproductive strategy is to produce fewer young and to look after each one carefully for a long period so it has a good chance of survival.

incubates them using its body heat. Some birds and reptiles bury their eggs in a warm place, such as sun-soaked sand or a mound of rotting vegetation.

Hatching is another hazardous stage. Predators may detect the movements, scents, or squawks of the hatchlings. However, many parents are at their most aggressive during this time and fight hard to defend their babies.

Pregnancy and birth

Unique to the animal world, mammal young develop to a fairly advanced stage before they leave their

Right Baby pheasants are not protected by their handsome looks; in the wild, there are many predators to avoid.

Below Horses, like other bigger animals, are pregnant for longer periods. This mare will produce her foal after about 11 months.

mother's body at birth. Their development takes place in a special part or organ inside the mother called the womb, or uterus.

The time between mating and birth is known as gestation or pregnancy. The bigger the mammal, the longer it tends to be. Some mice are pregnant for only 20 days, while elephants and certain whales carry their young inside them for almost 2 years. This is mainly because all babies start as a microscopic fertilized egg cell, so big babies need more time than small ones to grow in the womb.

In those mammals that are highly hunted, such as the wildebeest and zebras on the African grasslands, the birth is over within minutes. The newborn are at

a very advanced stage of development and are able to walk, then run, within an hour.

Mammals that have powerful weapons, such as the big cats and dogs, can give birth less hurriedly. Their babies are less at risk from predators, and the parents are well able to defend them. The new babies are usually in a relatively helpless state and need careful tending after birth.

Three types of mammals

Mammals get their name from the mammary glands that all female mammals possess. These glands produce milk to nourish the young after birth. Mammals are divided into three major groups based on their reproductive methods. These groups are called the monotremes, the marsupials, and the placentals.

The echidnas (spiny anteaters) and platypus are monotremes. The monotreme mother does not give birth to babies, but lays eggs. When the babies hatch from these, she feeds them on milk made in her mammary glands.

The marsupial group includes kangaroos, wallabies, koalas, and opossums. Their babies are born in a relatively early, immature state. In some cases, the babies' limbs have only just begun to form. The babies crawl to the mother's pocket or pouch. This is known as a marsupium and gives the group its name. There, they feed on her milk and continue their development.

Mammals within the placental group include many familiar creatures. Dogs, cats, horses, and monkeys, as well as marine mammals such as whales, dolphins, porpoises, seals, sea lions, and sea cows all belong to this diverse group. The babies develop

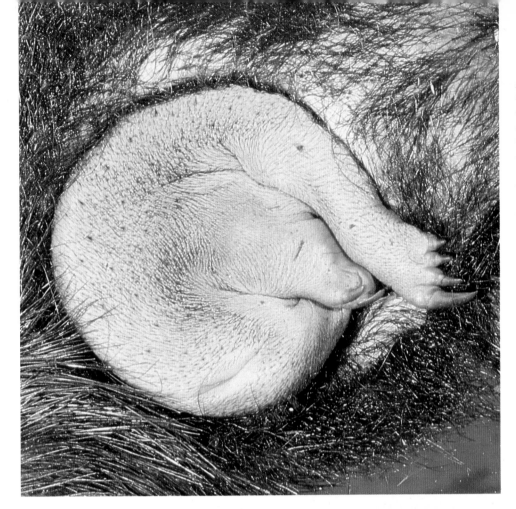

Left After the baby echidna hatches from its egg, it curls into the mother's pouch. There are only three species of egg-laying mammals – the "duck-billed" platypus and two kinds of echidna. They live only in Australia and Papua New Guinea.

Left This zebra foal is just a few minutes old, and still damp from embryonic bag and fluids. Yet it is already standing up and alert, ready to run.

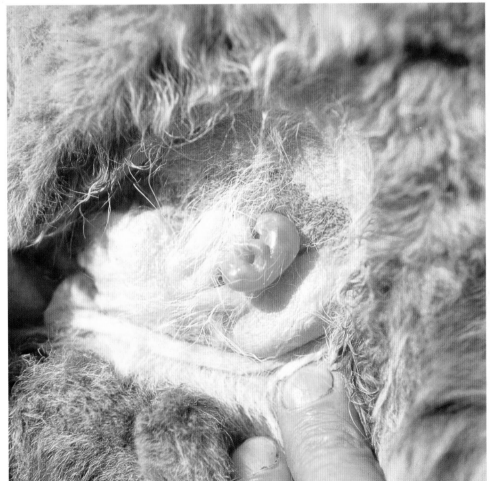

Right Do you recognize this animal baby? It is a newborn kangaroo attached to the teat in its mother's pouch. Marsupial babies are born at a very early stage in development. Placental mammals develop far beyond this stage in their mother's womb.

Right These newborn baby elephants grew inside their mother's womb for 22 months, nourished by her placenta (afterbirth). Compare their stage of development with that of the baby kangaroo on the previous page. It's hard to believe that they have been out of the womb for almost the same number of days.

Below The young mountain goat depends on its mother for protection, food, warmth, and comfort.

to a more advanced stage in the womb than young marsupials. They are nourished in the womb by a special part called the placenta or afterbirth, which transfers food from the mother's blood to the baby.

Baby care

The animals chosen for this book illustrate a wide variety of ways of looking after newborn babies. In some species, both parents care for the youngsters. In many species, this is the mother's role alone.

As with pregnancy, bigger animals tend to have a longer period of parental care. This is partly because the bigger youngsters take a longer time to grow to maturity. In monkeys, and particularly in apes such as the chimpanzee and gorilla, there is also a "childhood" period. During this time, the offspring are no longer dependent on their mother for milk, but they stay close by. They develop their complex patterns of behavior by watching, copying, experimenting, and learning from their elders.

Left Compared to mammals and birds, prolonged infant care is rare in invertebrates (animals without backbones). There are some exceptions, however, such as certain types of spiders and this burrowing scorpion with a piggyback-load of babies.

Habitats and their hazards

In this book, each species of animal is grouped with other species that share its habitat. A habitat is a characteristic place or type of landscape, such as a mountainside, tropical forest, river, or desert.

Grouping the animals in this way allows a closer look at the ways in which each species solves the problems posed by its particular habitat. These problems may include the climate, the availability of food and shelter, and the presence of predators.

MOTHER'S MILK AND WEANING

A mammal mother's milk is the complete food for her babies during their early stages. It contains energy, building-block nutrients for bodily growth, and vitamins and minerals for good health. It even contains natural chemicals, called antibodies, that help to protect the babies against certain infectious illnesses.

Mammal milk varies from one species to another, according to the babies' particular needs. For example, the milk of mother whales and seals is very rich in fats. These provide plenty of energy to enable the baby to keep up its body temperature in cold seas. The fats also provide the raw materials for the baby to build up its own heat-retaining layer of blubber under the skin.

Above A young springbok nurses from the teat. The mother remains watchful during this time, ever alert for lions and other predators.

POLAR REGIONS

Can you imagine being born into a world that is as cold as the inside of a deep freeze? The predominant color is the glaring white of snow and ice, but you cannot see it in the depths of winter because it is dark most of the day as well as at night. This is the world facing baby polar bears, penguin chicks, seal pups, and tiny lemmings. In most habitats, predators await the opportune moment to steal the youngsters as soon as the parents drop their guard. In this harshest of habitats, the intense cold, biting winds, and thick snow and ice claim many young.

Right The white fur of the new harp seal pup provides excellent camouflage in the snow and ice of the Far North.

Opposite As the pup grows, its fur becomes yellower. When it is a juvenile, the coat molts to light gray with dark brown spots and gradually develops the characteristic "harp" shape on the back.

Below Map showing the distribution of the polar regions and the featured animal species.

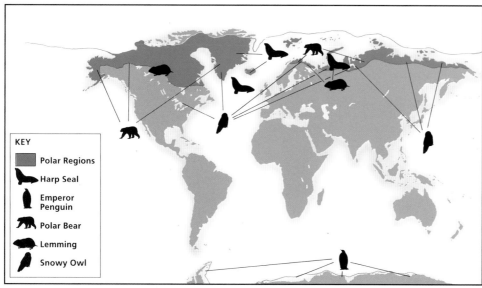

KEY

- Polar Regions
- Harp Seal
- Emperor Penguin
- Polar Bear
- Lemming
- Snowy Owl

HARP SEAL

*The snowy white harp seal pups spend
their first weeks on icebergs or rocky
islets before taking to the cold waters that
will be their home and larder.*

The newborn harp seal pup is one of the most endearing babies in the animal world. With big, black eyes and nose and a plump, white-furred body, it lies on the rocks or ice in complete and trusting innocence.

However, its childhood is a short one. Within a month of giving birth, the mother leaves to feed and restore her body reserves. The youngster is then forced by hunger to dive into the cold ocean and learn to fend for itself.

Migration to the south

Harp seals are representative species of the seal family, Phocidae. They are slow and awkward on land, but beautifully graceful and speedy in the water. They spend their summers in the icy seas and on the frozen coasts of the far north, in the Arctic. There they dive and chase their food. They hunt small shrimplike creatures, called krill, and fish, such as capelin and cod.

As summer merges into fall, the seals swim south along the coasts of southern Greenland, northeastern North America, northern Scandinavia and Asia, on a lengthy migration. By winter, they have reached their breeding grounds. These include the rocky coasts and ice floes along northeast Newfoundland, around the Gulf of St. Lawrence, on Jan Mayen island off Norway, and on the Beloye More, or White Sea, in northern Russia.

*Below A baby harp seal
drinks its mother's rich
milk as she rests on the ice.*

BABY FACTFILE

ANIMAL
Harp seal

SCIENTIFIC NAME
Phoca (Pagophilus) groenlandicus

DISTRIBUTION
*Northern seas and coasts
including the North Atlantic and
Arctic Oceans from Greenland to
northern Russia*

SIZE OF MOTHER
*Length 5-8 feet; weight 350-400
pounds*

LENGTH OF PREGNANCY
49 weeks

NUMBER OF BABIES
1 pup

SIZE AT BIRTH
Weight 20 pounds

EARLY DEVELOPMENT
*Feeds on rich mother's milk for
2-4 weeks, then mother leaves;
pup molts fur, learns to swim and
feed on fish and krill*

WHEN INDEPENDENT
4 weeks

WHEN ABLE TO BREED
*Females at 5 years, males at
4 years*

In February and March, the pregnant seal mothers gather by the thousands on the ice floes. Each defends a small patch of territory by grunting and pretending to bite her neighbors. Meanwhile, the males fight each other, using their teeth and flippers, for the right to mate with a female.

Around three weeks after arriving, the mother gives birth to her pup. The furry bundle lies on the ice and feeds on its thick, rich mother's milk. The pup's growth is astonishing – from 20 pounds at birth, it increases to a massively plump 70 pounds at only three weeks old! Its luxurious fur and a thick layer of fatty blubber under the skin keep the pup snug and warm on its icy nursery.

Providing so much nourishment places a huge burden on the mother, and she soon becomes thin and hungry. Between two and four weeks after giving birth, she dives into the waves to catch up on feeding. She also finds a male to mate with.

The male and female harp seals perform a graceful underwater ballet as they court. He calls and sings to her through the ocean before they mate. Afterward, the adult females continue to feed and prepare for their return journey northward.

Independent at one month

The harp seal pups are left on the ice floes by themselves. Their white fur changes to the adult pattern of light gray with brown spots. Hunger finally forces the pups into the water, where they learn to

Above *These endearing eyes will soon be spotting fish to catch and consume.*

catch krill and other food. They may have to dive to great depths when chasing prey. Their fur and blubber form a thick, warm wetsuit that keeps the core of the seal's body at a normal temperature.

The males, which are still in the area, provide some protection from predators such as orca and polar bears. Soon the pups are feeding regularly and are able to look after themselves. Then the whole seal herd is ready to migrate north for another summer in the high Arctic.

Desirable fur coats

The newborn harp seal pups are called whitecoats, and their fur is known as lanugo fur. This was once much prized for making fur coats for people. The sight of human hunters clubbing the baby seals to death, for the purpose of stripping them of their thick fur, caused much outrage. Today, such hunting has declined and is banned in some areas.

However, harp seals are still culled, or killed, to control population numbers. This is partly to stop them from eating huge amounts of fish, diminishing fishing catches. The harp seal is in little danger of extinction, however, because there are close to three million of them in the northern oceans.

EMPEROR PENGUIN

Emperor penguin chicks see almost nothing during their first weeks of life, except their parents, other chicks, and endless ice stretching on all sides.

Emperor penguins are the largest of the 16 kinds of penguins. Like the others, they cannot fly but are expert swimmers, with wings like paddles.

The emperor penguin chick hatches into one of the most inhospitable places on Earth: an ice shelf in the Antarctic, in the middle of winter. Winds blow at 50 miles per hour. The temperature is minus 4°F and that is the average – it sometimes gets colder! It is the coldest, darkest, windiest nursery you can imagine.

The main reason that emperor penguins breed in such extreme conditions is probably lack of predators. Few predatory animals can withstand the cold, so there is little risk of the babies being eaten. However, the cold that keeps predators at bay may also prove fatal for the chicks.

Gathering on the ice

As the Antarctic winter approaches, in April and May, adult emperor penguins gather on pack ice around the great southern continent of Antarctica. They pair up, male with female, and mate. The mother lays a single egg and then returns to the penguin's natural home, the sea. There she swims and dives effortlessly after shrimp, fish, and squid.

The father is left with the egg through the depths of winter. It is bitterly cold and so far south that there

Above *The tiny emperor penguin chick dozes while sitting on the feet of its parent. The adult keeps an eye on its youngster while preening its own plumage.*

Below *While both parents are feeding at sea, the chicks gather into unaccompanied nursery groups. Predators are rare so far south.*

BABY FACTFILE

ANIMAL
Emperor penguin

SCIENTIFIC NAME
Aptenodytes forsteri

DISTRIBUTION
Southern oceans and Antarctica, pack ice

SIZE OF MOTHER
Height 4 feet

LENGTH OF INCUBATION
9 weeks

NUMBER OF BABIES
1 egg

SIZE AT BIRTH
12-14 inches

EARLY DEVELOPMENT
Chick is fed by father, then mother, then both; molts baby feathers after 6-8 weeks

WHEN INDEPENDENT
8-10 weeks

WHEN ABLE TO BREED
1-2 years

Left *This older chick is preparing to beg for food from the adults. What to us would be a smelly, revolting meal of half-digested fish, squid, and other small sea life is greedily gobbled up.*

is hardly any daylight. Having no food, he must live on the reserves of fat stored in his body.

There are no materials to build a nest. The father must incubate the egg, or keep it warm, by holding it on his feet and covering it with a special flap of body flesh, skin, and feathers on his belly. If he leaves the egg, even for a few minutes, it will freeze. So the father must stand there for weeks, huddled with hundreds of other males against the weather.

After about 64 days, the chick hatches. It is covered with a very fluffy set of downy feathers for protection against the ice and biting wind. The father feeds it on a pasty fluid from his crop, or storage stomach. Dads and chicks crowd together, two to every square foot, for warmth and protection.

Eventually the female returns. The area of ice has increased through the winter, and she may have to walk over 50 miles from the open sea to the breeding site. But she is well fed and able to take over the baby-sitting duties. The father sets off for the ocean,

having last eaten more than 100 days ago.

From then on, the mother and father take turns to feed and guard the chick, and feed themselves in the sea. Gradually spring approaches. There is more daylight, and the pack ice begins to break up.

Penguin nursery

When the chick is about six weeks old, both parents leave it for short periods. Many chicks huddle together in groups like nurseries, as parents come and go. Each mother and father can pick out their own chick, from the hundreds milling around, by its squawky calls.

Between about six and eight weeks after hatching the chick sheds its fluffy down feathers. These are replaced by the adult plumage of sleek white front, yellow neck, and black back and flipper-wings. The young penguin soon learns to swim and feed beneath the waves. But it is a long, hard childhood. Only one chick in five survives to the first birthday.

POLAR BEAR

*Polar bear cubs are nursed by their
mother in an ice den before they begin
their wandering life across the seas,
snows, and pack ice of the Arctic.*

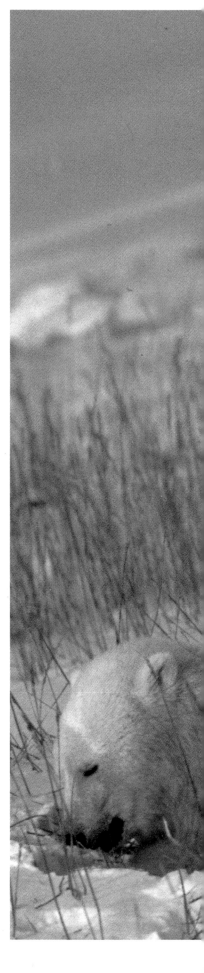

The birth of a polar bear is great news for a zoo. People flock to see this cuddliest of cubs with its huge, powerful mother in attendance.

Although the polar bear mother and baby are a heart-warming sight, the natural land of the polar bear is anything but warm. These massive hunters live at the limits of endurance, along the oceans and seas on the far fringes of the polar basin. For the first three months of its life, a baby polar bear sees little except the inside of its snow den, its mother, and its brother or sister. Not until spring does it emerge into the lengthening daylight and look around at the dazzling snowscape.

The cuddly cub will grow up to be the most carnivorous, or meat eating, of all the bears. The polar bear's preferred prey are ringed seals, bearded seals, and walruses, but they also feed on carrion, such as a beached whale or walrus, and crabs and fish that have washed ashore. Polar bears gorge on berries and fruits in late summer, and they may eat sea birds, their eggs and chicks, hares, and caribou (reindeer).

Apart from mothers with cubs, polar bears live alone. During a long breeding season from March through July, females and males pair up briefly, and mate with little ceremony. In late fall or early winter, the female seeks out a suitable snowfall or drift, up

BABY FACTFILE

ANIMAL
Polar bear, sea bear

SCIENTIFIC NAME
Ursus (*or* Thalarctos) maritimus

DISTRIBUTION
*Lands, islands, and ice floes
around Arctic Ocean (Russia,
Norway, Greenland, Canada, and
Alaska)*

SIZE OF MOTHER
*Length of head and body 7-8 feet;
weight 500-600 pounds*

LENGTH OF PREGNANCY
30-39 weeks

NUMBER OF BABIES
1-4 cubs, usually 2

SIZE AT BIRTH
Length 1 foot; weight 20-25 ounces

EARLY DEVELOPMENT
*Slow development, with ears and
eyes not open until several weeks
after birth*

WHEN INDEPENDENT
About 2 years, rarely less

WHEN ABLE TO BREED
*Females at 4-6 years, males at
3-5 years*

Left Twin cubs follow
their sow mother across a
sandy beach as she sniffs
the ground in search of
food.

Right The mother guards
her cubs vigilantly and will
charge at any intruder.

Right The bear family picks its way between the pools and bogs of the snowmelt.

Opposite Note the huge size of this four-month-old cub's paws and claws. They will be effective strike-to-kill weapons in the future.

against a hill or rock. There she digs out the den where she will give birth in deep midwinter, December or January.

It was once thought that polar bears, and other bears, hibernated during the winter. Scientists now believe that bears do not undergo true hibernation, with a drastic fall in body temperature. Instead, they have a period of dormancy or deep sleep, during which the body temperature falls only a few degrees. They can rouse themselves if necessary – for instance, to wander outside the den and have a snack during a mild spell.

The mother polar bear also rouses herself to give birth to her cubs, usually two. She feeds her babies on milk, cares for them, and sleeps between times. Outside the den, it is desperately cold, with bone-chilling winds, ice and snow, and long, dark nights.

Slow development

The newborn bears have sparse, short, whitish fur, and their eyes and ears are closed. They do not walk until at least a month old. Although they begin to hear at about three or four weeks, their ears are not working well until about ten weeks of age. Their eyes open at four or five weeks.

A special feature of their mother's milk is its high fat content – almost one-third. The babies use this fat largely as a source of energy to keep up their body temperatures in the cold surroundings. By the time the cubs leave the den, usually in March or April, they have grown to about 20 pounds in weight. During their first summer, the cubs watch and learn as their mother stalks and hunts, and they share her meals of seal meat or fish. She continues to nurse the cubs for two years. Thereafter, the mother

discourages their attempts to rely on her. The youngsters must now hunt for their survival.

Suited to an icy world

Polar bears are well adapted to survive in their icy home. A guard coat of coarse hairs and a dense underfur keep out the intense cold. Additional protection comes from a layer of fat or blubber just under the skin. This fat is up to 3 inches thick around the hips and back legs. It also gives the bear buoyancy, so that it can stay afloat and swim more easily. Oils in the fur repel water so that the coat does not become waterlogged.

The whitish color of the fur gives ideal camouflage in the snowy landscape. The polar bear even has fur on the soles of its feet, between the foot pads. This allows the bear to move across ice and snow without slipping. Polar bears are surprisingly fast runners, and can sprint for short distances at speeds reaching almost 20 miles per hour. They are excellent swimmers and divers, swimming as far as 60 miles at about 6 miles per hour, before resting.

The mother and her cubs are nomads with no home base. They wander for miles, catching any food they can and resting in sheltered spots during the worst weather. In northern Canada, migrating bears will wander through communities. If a bear becomes a nuisance, it is trapped and relocated.

By the age of about two years, the cubs have grown big and strong and weigh some 300 pounds. Although they can fend for themselves, they often seem reluctant to leave their mother. But the mother knows that she will be unable to feed new cubs, and perhaps even herself, with other full-grown bears around, so she may actively chase them away.

LEMMING

*Small and vulnerable, lemmings survive
mainly by breeding and completing their
life cycle before predators can
consume them.*

Lemmings are small, furry creatures resembling mice and voles. According to legend, lemmings breed so quickly that every few years they become too numerous. Then huge groups of them set off, scuttling over the landscape like a moving, lumpy, long-pile carpet. They head for the nearest cliff, riverbank, or seashore – and leap to their deaths by the thousand.

Like most animal legends, this story is partly true. Lemmings really do set off on long treks when they become very numerous. As they multiply in a local area, individuals meet each other more often. There are fewer places to shelter, and food becomes scarce. These factors trigger the lemmings' wandering instincts. But their intention is not suicide – it is survival. They migrate in the hope of finding new areas with plentiful food and living space.

The bands of migrating lemmings get funneled and channeled by features of the landscape, such as steep hills and streams. Gradually they come together into huge marching "armies." If the lemmings' route leads to a steep cliff or a body of water, their instincts are so strong that they press on, jumping or swimming in an attempt to reach the other side. Sadly, most perish.

However, this is just one possible future for a litter of baby lemmings. They are born in a nest of dried grass in an underground burrow. It is spring, but so

BABY FACTFILE

ANIMAL
Lemming

SCIENTIFIC NAME
Dicrostonyx, Lemmus, *and others
(9 species)*

DISTRIBUTION
*Tundra, woods, and grasslands of
the northern North Hemisphere*

SIZE OF MOTHER
*Length of head and body 5
inches, tail 1 inch; weight 1 ounce*

LENGTH OF PREGNANCY
3 weeks

NUMBER OF BABIES
*3-9 young per litter, several litters
in good years*

SIZE AT BIRTH
*Length ½ inch; weight 1/30th
ounce*

EARLY DEVELOPMENT
Helpless, with eyes closed at birth

WHEN INDEPENDENT
3-4 weeks

WHEN ABLE TO BREED
*Females at 4-6 weeks, males at 6-8
weeks*

Below *The collared
lemming mother moves
her young after their nest
area has been disturbed.
She carries them by the
scruff of the neck.*

far north that snow still covers the ground. The snow forms a blanket that keeps out the chilling winds and severe night frosts. Adult lemmings make tunnels beneath the snow to reach the mosses, grasses, and other plants that they eat throughout the year.

Like most small rodents, new lemmings are helpless at birth, with eyelids still closed. They do little except feed on their mother's milk, wriggle, squeak, and sleep. The mother lemming is very protective. As the babies grow and become able to crawl from the nest, she runs out and carries them back to safety.

Always on the go

Spring lengthens and the snows thaw. By three weeks of age, the babies are able to leave the nest and begin gnawing on plants. They feed both day and night, stopping only for short intervals to rest. The young and adults must be constantly on the alert. Weasels,

Above *This young lemming is well enough developed to leave the nest and explore a new world of scents, sights, sounds, and whiskery touch sensations.*

owls and hawks, foxes and wildcats, ravens, and skuas and other seabirds are always ready to grab a lemming snack. The lemmings rely chiefly on their senses of smell and hearing to warn of predators.

Each lemming has a small territory that it defends against neighbors, using a variety of squeaks and other sounds. The babies share their mother's territory at first, but soon they must claim their own patches of land. Less than two months after birth, a lemming is fully grown and ready to raise its own family – one of the shortest childhoods in the mammal world!

SNOWY OWL

Snowy owl chicks are carefully groomed, fed, and protected in the nest by their hardworking parents until they take their first twilight flights.

With their huge eyes and extraordinarily sensitive ears, owls are typical creatures of the night. They flit through the darkness on powerful wings with soft-edged feathers. When an owl locates prey, it swoops down and grasps it in powerful talons, or claws, then returns to the roost to feed.

This description – except for the part about the night – fits the snowy owl of the far north. Snowy owls tend to hunt in the day, and during the twilight of dawn and dusk. They rarely venture forth at night.

The male snowy owl is almost all white, with a few flecks on the wings. The larger female has dark

Left A young snowy owl opens its fearsome beak slightly in a defensive half-threat.

BABY FACTFILE

ANIMAL
Snowy owl

SCIENTIFIC NAME
Nyctea scandiaca

DISTRIBUTION
On tundra, moors, marshes, and islands in the far north of North America, Greenland, Europe, and Asia

SIZE OF MOTHER
Length of head and body 20-25 inches

LENGTH OF INCUBATION
4-5 weeks

NUMBER OF EGGS
4-10, up to 15 in a good year

SIZE AT BIRTH
Length 3-4 inches

EARLY DEVELOPMENT
Newly hatched are helpless with downy feathers; stay in nest for 3 weeks; fly at 5-6 weeks

WHEN INDEPENDENT
8-12 weeks

WHEN ABLE TO BREED
2-3 years

brown bars on her upper parts and sometimes on her underparts. However, she is still mainly white, making her beautifully camouflaged in the snow and ice of winter, and against the pale gray skies.

Snowy owls catch a variety of food, chiefly lemmings, mice, voles, rabbits, hares, and ground squirrels. They have also been seen hunting birds such as buntings, oystercatchers, ducks, and even gulls and skuas, as well as the occasional fish and large insects.

Rudimentary nest

Snowy owls follow the owl tradition of being poor nest builders. The pair court and mate in spring, and the female lays her eggs in a simple hollow or scrape in the ground. Or she may use a rock, lined with moss and feathers.

The nest site has a good view so that the female can keep watch as she sits on the eggs to keep them warm. The male catches food for himself and his partner. In between hunting trips, he also keeps watch. If danger looms, he gives an alarm call of a harsh *kik* bark and snaps his beak.

The female begins to sit on the eggs, or incubate them, when she lays the first one. She lays the second egg a day or so later, and so on. Since all the eggs have the same incubation period, they hatch in the

Above *The immature snowy owl has dark barred feathers, which help to camouflage it against the summer landscape. It will molt to almost pure white.*

same sequence. The first-born chick is bigger than the others and, if food runs short, it may eat the smallest.

The new babies have sparse down, and look thin and spindly. Soon they grow fluffier, slate-gray down feathers. Each chick needs the equivalent of two lemmings daily, so both parents hunt to feed the appetites of their family. The parents tear their catches into bits to give to their young.

Mob protection

The chicks keep very still when their parents are away from the nest. Although they are out in the open, they are very difficult to spot because they look like a pile of rounded rocks. If a predator comes near, the mother and father fly to attack and frustrate its pursuit.

The chicks stay in the nest for about three weeks. Then their adult flight feathers grow, and by six weeks they are practicing in the air. Like other owls, the young stay with their parents for some time, often into the fall.

CONIFEROUS FORESTS

In the lands of the Far North, vast dark green belts of forest stretch around the world. Some of the trees in the forests are pines, firs, and spruces. Their seeds grow in woody cones, so they are called "conifers." They are evergreens, keeping their leaves year-round. But in winter, forests are not green but white. Deep snows blanket the land, and life becomes difficult for the creatures living there. So caribou, squirrels, and wolves tend to raise their babies during the gentler days of the short summer.

Right *A wolf pup laps cautiously.*

Opposite *Mother and pup relax in a safe, secluded place among the forest undergrowth.*

Below *Map showing the distribution of the coniferous forests and the featured animal species.*

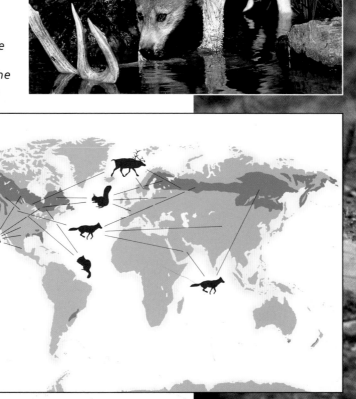

KEY

Coniferous Forests

Gray Wolf

Caribou

Red Squirrel

Eastern Chipmunk

Striped Skunk

GRAY WOLF

A wolf pup is brought up in a well-organized social group, or pack, and learns to communicate by body language and a variety of sounds.

Have you ever seen a newborn puppy? It is small, chubby, and helpless, with short fur and eyelids closed. A newborn wolf pup looks much the same. Indeed, wolves and dogs are similar in many ways. This is not surprising, since all breeds of domestic dogs are believed to have descended from wolves.

Baby wolves are usually born in late winter. For the first few weeks, they stay in the den, which is a hollow, cave, or rock shelter that the mother uses regularly. She feeds her pups with milk from the teats on her belly.

Opposite *The young wolf pup is a picture of fluffy innocence.*

Below *An adult wolf preparing to pick up and carry a cub by the scruff of its neck.*

BABY FACTFILE

ANIMAL
Gray wolf (timber wolf and other names)

SCIENTIFIC NAME
Canis lupus

DISTRIBUTION
Forests, plains, and wilderness areas of North America, Europe, Middle East, and Asia

SIZE OF MOTHER
Length of head and body 4 feet, tail up to 2 feet; weight 50-75 pounds

LENGTH OF PREGNANCY
9 weeks

NUMBER OF BABIES
4-7 pups

SIZE AT BIRTH
Length about 6–8 inches

EARLY DEVELOPMENT
Pups are born blind and helpless; eyes open after 9 days; leave den after 1 month; travel with pack at 3-5 months

WHEN INDEPENDENT
About 1 year

WHEN ABLE TO BREED
Females at 2 years, males at 3 years

The pups' eyes open after nine or ten days. Their short fur is sooty brown. If they and their mother are healthy and well fed, they will have rolls of "puppy fat." Soon they are learning to stand and walk.

Wolves are very social animals and usually live in extended family groups, called packs. The number in a pack varies with the amount of food available, from 3 or 4 to more than 20 animals. About 3 or 4 weeks after the birth, the youngsters venture from the den. It is then that they meet the other pack members.

The pack members are friendly to the young pups and all share in their care and protection. The mother and other wolves bring the pups food, and the youngsters practice eating and chewing. They also tumble, roll, and play with each other and with other family members.

Wolf manners

Hunting as a group, gray wolves can kill prey as large as moose and caribou. On their own, they take beavers, hares, rabbits, mice and voles, and birds and their eggs. In some areas, they also raid trash cans and dumps. As the pups grow bigger and stronger, they learn about catching food and "wolf talk."

In the pack, there is an order of seniority, called a pack hierarchy. This ranges from the chief adults, the mother and father, who generally pair for life, down to the younger, junior wolves. The pack members communicate their place in the hierarchy by whines, yips, howls, and snarls, and also by the movements and positions of their face, ears, body, and tail. For example, a senior wolf bares its teeth and stands tall, with tail up. A junior wolf responds by flattening its ears, cowering down, and lowering its tail.

Gradually the young wolves become full pack members and take their place in the hierarchy. As a junior wolf becomes bigger and stronger, it may challenge for a more senior position. Or it may leave its pack and join another. If it rises through the ranks to become a pack leader, it can raise pups of its own.

CARIBOU

*Born during migration, the young caribou
has to follow the herd almost from birth
or be left to the wolves and bears.*

Groups of caribou roam the northern lands of Canada, Alaska, and Siberia. These deer are alert and wary, ever watchful for predators. They listen and sniff as they feed, and occasionally a group member raises its head to scan the landscape. Wolves are a constant threat, some packs following the same caribou groups for months or years. They single out the weak, the sick, the old, and the very young.

A typical caribou group consists of adult females with their young. Many males, especially older ones, live alone or on the outskirts of the female groups. Males and females may form loose bands for migration. Some groups move between winter grounds in the forests and wood edges to the south, and summer feeding areas on the treeless tundra to the far north. Other caribou groups migrate over a shorter distance.

Nearly all the baby caribou, called calves, are born within two or three weeks, often in June. This avoids the remnants of bad weather from the previous winter and gives them sufficient time to grow strong during the summer. The babies are well developed at birth and look like small versions of their parents, except they lack antlers.

The migrating group does not stop during the birth, but moves on, covering up to 20 miles each day. Mother and newborn must not get left behind. The mother stands in front of baby, bobs her head up and down, and makes grunting sounds, signaling that the calf must get up and go with her. A new calf can trot in less than an hour and sprint faster than a human when only three or four hours old.

When an enemy appears, the whole group panics and gallops off. Sometimes babies are separated from their mothers, but they are soon reunited, recogniz-

Below Almost as soon as the young caribou is born, it must follow the herd on migration. This means steady walking, with the occasional run – and sometimes wading and swimming across streams and rivers.

BABY FACTFILE

ANIMAL
Caribou, reindeer

SCIENTIFIC NAME
Rangifer tarandus

DISTRIBUTION
Around the northern lands of North America, Europe, and Asia

SIZE OF MOTHER
Height 3-4 feet at shoulder; length of head and body 5-6 feet; weight 200-300 pounds (reindeer usually smaller)

LENGTH OF PREGNANCY
30-36 weeks

NUMBER OF BABIES
Usually 1, occasionally 2

SIZE AT BIRTH
Height 16-20 inches; weight 8-10 pounds

EARLY DEVELOPMENT
Baby is well developed at birth and runs with the herd 1 or 2 hours later

WHEN INDEPENDENT
8-12 months

WHEN ABLE TO BREED
1-3 years

Left *This caribou baby, lying quietly in the long grass, is about one month old. Its antlers will not appear for several weeks, but their sites are marked by tufts of darker fur.*

ing each other mainly by scent. Mother and baby also bleat to each other if danger is near.

Unusual deer

After about a month, the young caribou begin to eat plants, though they will continue to suckle their mother's milk for several more months. In summer, they feed on the tundra growths of grasses, sedges, soft buds and twigs, horsetails, mosses, and other plants.

Caribou are unique among deer in that both males and females have antlers, although those of the male are usually larger. At three or four months of age, young caribou begin to grow their antlers. These first appear as tiny "spike horns." By then fall is approaching and the group migrates back to the south. Like most deer, they have a rut in the fall. The males bellow and battle each other to win the right to mate with females.

The caribou is also the only deer without a bare patch on the muzzle. This is furred, presumably to keep in body warmth during the cold and snows of winter. The cloven-hoofed foot is very broad and acts as a wide "snowshoe" for walking over soft snow or through bogs.

In winter, the caribou eat whatever they can. They scrape away snow to find ground plants and browse on twigs and buds, such as aspen and willow, and soft bark.

The caribou and the reindeer of Europe and Greenland can breed together, and so are included as one species. But reindeer are generally slightly smaller and easier to domesticate, or tame, than caribou. Caribou are still hunted by sportspeople and Native Americans, who use parts of the body for meat, clothing, boat covers, tents, tools, and implements. European Lapps herd reindeer and similarly depend on their milk, meat, hides, bones, and antlers, as well as the tourist trade this attracts.

RED SQUIRREL

Baby red squirrels are relatively safe in their stick nest, or drey, but life becomes more risky when they start to scamper through the treetops.

How many kinds, or species, do you think there are in the squirrel family around the world? The answer is nearly 250! The squirrel family includes marmots, woodchucks or groundhogs, prairie dogs, and chipmunks, all of which live mainly on the ground. But many squirrels, including the red squirrels, are slim, agile tree dwellers. They have bright eyes, gripping claws on their hands and feet, and long bushy tails. Few are more attractive than the red squirrels, with their chestnut-red fur, white chests, and neat, pricked and tufted ears.

Red squirrels do not look so bright-eyed and bushy-tailed when they are born. They seem to have left their mother's womb too early. The babies are indistinct pink blobs with no fur, no teeth, and eyes closed. They are cared for by their mother in a nest she has built from leaves, twigs, and sticks. The nest is called a drey and is usually high in a tree fork. It is lined with soft mosses and stems, and is often ball shaped with a small entrance hole. The female squirrel builds several dreys in her neighborhood. Few predators can reach into the high branches, but if one is near, the mother quickly moves her young. She carries them by the scruff of the neck to another, safer drey.

The tiny babies feed on their mother's milk and continue to develop. Their fur begins to grow by about two weeks of age. At three weeks, their lower front teeth appear. Their eyes open at about four

Below Only a few days old, these babies still have closed eyes.

Opposite A youngster gets the feel of balancing on a branch.

BABY FACTFILE

ANIMAL
Red squirrel

SCIENTIFIC NAME
Tamiasciurus hudsonicus (American), Sciurus vulgaris (European)

DISTRIBUTION
Northern forests, chiefly coniferous forests

SIZE OF MOTHER
Length of head and body 7-8 inches, tail 4-6 inches

LENGTH OF PREGNANCY
5-7 weeks

NUMBER OF BABIES
Average 3 in a litter, 2 litters a year

SIZE AT BIRTH
Length about 1 inch; weight $^1/_4$-$^1/_2$ ounce

EARLY DEVELOPMENT
Babies have neither teeth nor fur and eyes are closed; fur appears at 10-13 days; teeth appear from 20 days; eyes open by 30 days; emerge from nest at 56 days

WHEN INDEPENDENT
3-4 months

WHEN ABLE TO BREED
1 year

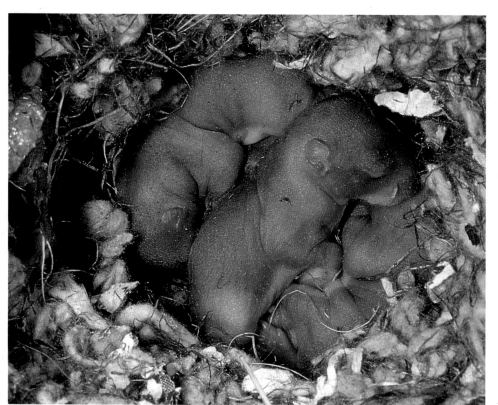

Above *As its eyes begin to open, the young red squirrel crawls and peers from its nest hole. Note the long, manipulating fingers on the forepaws.*

Opposite *The interior of the drey, or nest, is soft and warm, lined with grasses and other vegetation.*

weeks, and the upper front teeth come through by five weeks. The babies' front teeth will become their vital feeding tools.

All squirrels belong to a group of mammals called rodents. The group also contains beavers, rats, mice, gophers, and similar creatures. The rodent's hallmark is its large, chisel-shaped front teeth, known as incisors. They are excellent gnawing teeth, and they continue to grow throughout life. So the incisors are always sharp and ready to slice bark, cut wood, and crack nuts and seeds.

The young squirrels begin to come out of their nest at eight or nine weeks of age. By then it is spring or summer, and they are ready to move from mother's milk to adult foods. Red squirrels eat a varied menu including nuts, seeds, fruit, conifer shoots and cones, insects, and fungi. They hold the food in their front paws, while sitting back on their haunches.

Young squirrels can open a nut by instinct – the behavior is built-in from birth. They nibble a hole in the shell and then insert the incisor teeth into it. Using the incisors as a lever, they then crack open the case. Some nuts have already been eaten and spoiled inside by grubs and maggots. The youngsters must learn how to recognize these nuts by trial and error.

They also begin to hide or bury food for eating later. Again, this behavior is instinctive, but their caching improves with practice. They bury the nuts

singly, just under the surface. Later they sniff them out, even those buried by another squirrel!

Learning to climb

Squirrels have very good eyesight to detect danger and sensitive whiskers to feel their way. The youngsters learn how to grip branches and bark, and leap from tree to tree. They can turn their feet right around, so they can hang upside down from a bough or trunk.

The bushy tail is not for show. It is a rudder to help the squirrel balance and turn as it jumps. It also acts as a flag for signaling to other squirrels. Wrapped around its owner, it is a whole-body scarf that keeps the squirrel warm while asleep.

EASTERN CHIPMUNK

Cheeky and cheerful in appearance, the young chipmunk is very curious as it investigates its surroundings for possible foods.

Familiar to many of us, this cheeky opportunist is bold and always ready to accept a tidbit at the woodland picnic site. The chipmunk now also lives in other countries, but not in the wild. It is one of the many types of small rodents kept as pets.

The chipmunk's bright eyes and furry tail are reminiscent of the squirrel's, and chipmunks are members of the squirrel family. Unlike most squirrels, chipmunks live mainly on or under the ground in burrows.

Helpless in the nest

The chipmunk's breeding season begins in February or April, when males seek out females in their burrows among the roots and rocks of the birch and pine woods. The babies are born about 31 days after mating, deep in the mother's system of burrows. They lie, tiny and helpless, in a snug nest of dry grass, leaves, and other plant material.

The newborns' eyelids are closed and their teeth have not yet appeared above the gums. The young chipmunks spend four weeks in the nest, with the female attending to their every need. She licks and grooms them, feeds them on her milk, and cleans away their droppings.

Outside their burrows, chipmunks are hunted by numerous predators. Bobcats, lynx, coyotes, foxes,

Below A hand-reared chipmunk guzzles milk from a dropper.

BABY FACTFILE

ANIMAL
Eastern chipmunk, chipmunk

SCIENTIFIC NAME
Tamias striatus

DISTRIBUTION
Forests of northern and eastern North America

SIZE OF MOTHER
Length of head and body 5-6 inches, tail 3-4 inches; weight 2-5 ounces

LENGTH OF PREGNANCY
4-5 weeks

NUMBER OF BABIES
2-8

SIZE AT BIRTH
Length 1-2 inches

EARLY DEVELOPMENT
Born toothless and with eyes closed; spend 4 weeks in nest; weaned at 5 weeks

WHEN INDEPENDENT
5-8 weeks

WHEN ABLE TO BREED
About 1 year

Above *Like most young animals, this chipmunk examines almost everything as possible food, and learns about smells and tastes.*

weasels, owls, and hawks all catch them. Even inside the burrow system, the mother and babies are not safe. Weasels and certain snakes are small enough to enter the tunnels.

Emerging for food

After about a month, the young chipmunks are able to leave the nest and forage for food. They come out in the early morning to search for nuts, berries, fruits, and seeds. They also feed on small animals such as worms, snails, slugs, insects, and, occasionally, little lizards, snakes, small mice, and even birds' eggs. By five weeks of age, the young chipmunks are no longer feeding on their mother's milk. However, they usually stay with her for several weeks longer.

Eventually it is time for the almost-grown chipmunks to begin life on their own. Each chipmunk digs a burrow under roots, logs, stones, and turf, where it sleeps at night and takes shelter from danger.

The main tunnel has several entrances and chambers, one of which is lined with grass and leaves as a nest.

Sometimes a chipmunk is fortunate enough to inherit a burrow. Then it digs to enlarge and improve its home. This busy rodent continues to tunnel throughout its life, and its burrows may reach over 30 feet long.

Making larders for winter

The chipmunk is famous for gathering and storing food for the long winter months. These stores, called caches, contain dry items such as nuts and hard seeds. There are usually several caches at different sites within the chipmunk's burrow system. Many smaller ones are scattered around its home range, under lumps of turf, stones, and logs. The chipmunk carries the food items in its cheek pouches, and can fit in up to four nuts on each side.

During winter, the chipmunk may sleep for several days at a time. However, like the squirrel, it does not truly hibernate. It can rouse itself to feed on cached food, and it may even wander from its burrow on mild winter days.

STRIPED SKUNK

Newborn skunks, like many other
newborn mammals, are tiny and hairless.
But the typical black-and-white
coloration is already in their skin.

In some areas people frequently come across skunks, but few go very close to them. Skunks are feared, not for any physical harm they may do but for the chemical harm. Their infamous trick is to turn the rear end toward an enemy and spray a terrible-smelling fluid from two anal glands at the base of the tail. The smell is so awful that it takes the enemy's breath away, and the fluid may cause temporary blindness if it gets into the eyes. The animals that suffer this attack rarely disturb a skunk again. They learn and recognize the skunk's vivid black-and-white markings, which are warning coloration, and leave it well alone.

As a warning before the spray, the skunk usually lowers its head, raises its tail, and stamps with its front paws. It may also do a handstand. If this fails, it squirts the attacker from up to 12 feet away.

Skunks are members of the weasel family, the mustelids. Skunks live in several types of habitat, such as dry scrubland, woods, and prairie. They may also live around and under outbuildings in country areas. Their range stretches from southern Canada down to northern Mexico.

Each skunk has a burrow where it rests during the day, emerging at night to feed. The den may be in a bank, under an old log, among rocks or roots, or under a woodpile or building. As the skunks prepare for breeding, the males in an area battle with each

BABY FACTFILE

ANIMAL
Striped skunk; skunk, common skunk

SCIENTIFIC NAME
Mephitis mephitis

DISTRIBUTION
Woods and open country in North America

SIZE OF MOTHER
Length of head and body 13-18 inches, tail 7-10 inches; weight 6-14 pounds

LENGTH OF PREGNANCY
About 9 weeks

NUMBER OF BABIES
Usually 5-6 kits

SIZE AT BIRTH
Weight 1 ounce

EARLY DEVELOPMENT
Newborn are toothless with no fur; eyes open at 21 days; weaned at 6-7 weeks

WHEN INDEPENDENT
6-8 months

WHEN ABLE TO BREED
1 year

Below Growing youngsters follow their mother and learn about the ways of the world as they forage and select edible items.

Left *The young skunk displays the vivid coloration that will warn molesters about its chemical defensive weapon – the vile-smelling, eye-stinging fluid sprayed from the base of the tail.*

other. Their fights cause a lot of noise and commotion, but few injuries. The winning males mate with the local females. After a pregnancy of 62 to 66 days, the females give birth to their babies, called kits. They are born in the mother's burrow.

The new kits are completely dependent on their mother. Their eyelids are closed, and they have no teeth. They also have no fur, but the typical black-and-white fur pattern of the adult skunk shows as a pattern in the kits' skin.

The babies feed on milk from their mother and grow rapidly. Their eyelids open at about 21 days. After another week or two, the mother takes her kits on feeding trips. If they lag behind, she picks them up and carries them by the scruff of the neck.

Varied menu

While many animals have a varied diet, the skunk has one of the most adaptable of all. Its range of foods includes all kinds of small creatures, from mice to insects, including grasshoppers, crickets, caterpillars, and beetles. The skunk also eats eggs, frogs, small birds, crayfish, and fish; it also sniffs out carrion. Sometimes it raids chicken coops, kills the chickens, and steals the eggs. In the fall, the skunk will fatten up on plant foods such as leaves, seeds, nuts, and berries.

Spraying danger

By the fall, the young skunks have grown up and they leave their mother. The skunk is mainly a solitary animal, and each young must set up its own territory and acquire its own den. In winter, though, the young skunks may share dens while they sleep for long periods.

The young skunks face several dangers. Pumas and bobcats hunt them when desperate enough to put up with the horrible-smelling spray. The great horned owl swoops on them, seeming to disregard the spray. Also, many skunks are killed on the roads at night. Instead of running away at the approach of a motor vehicle, they stand their ground and spray. But the spray is no defense against a speeding automobile.

TEMPERATE FORESTS

Conditions are rarely harsh in the temperate woodlands. Winters are cold, but not endlessly freezing, while summers are warm, but not scorched and parched. The trees and flowers provide a multitude of foods, such as juicy buds, leaves, blossoms, fruits, and nuts. Trees also give shelter from the worst of the wind and rain. And they furnish a variety of hiding places around their roots, in tree-trunk holes, and among the twigs and leaves. Life is regular and seasonal for the animals that raise their families in this generally milder habitat. They include many of our favorite and familiar creatures, such as the red fox and white-tailed deer.

Opposite *A mother grizzly rears up on her hind legs to survey the landscape in a clearing among the trees, and one of the cubs attempts to copy her.*

Right *A three-month-old grizzly bear cub peers quizzically at the camera – bears are relatively shortsighted – as it noses about in the leaf litter of the forest floor.*

Right *Map showing the distribution of the temperate forests and the featured animal species.*

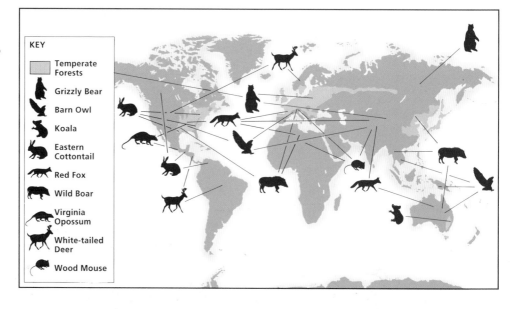

KEY

- Temperate Forests
- Grizzly Bear
- Barn Owl
- Koala
- Eastern Cottontail
- Red Fox
- Wild Boar
- Virginia Opossum
- White-tailed Deer
- Wood Mouse

GRIZZLY BEAR

The huge adult grizzly bear is more powerful than several people together, but the baby grizzly is tiny and helpless.

Above *A tiny ten-day-old cub crawls in its mother's thick fur.*

Newborn bear cubs are tiny compared to their mothers. A new baby grizzly bear weighs as little as 10 ounces, while its mother may be well over 400 pounds. The cubs are helpless at birth with closed eyes and no fur or teeth. They spend many weeks growing and developing in the mother's den. The babies may not emerge into the wide world until they are over three months old.

Growing fat in the fall

Bears are solitary animals. The male and female come together for only a week or two, in early summer, to court and mate. Then they separate and continue their solitary lives.

Grizzlies are great opportunists and eat a wide variety of food, from soft leaves and buds to roots

Left *The cubs at six months of age.*

BABY FACTFILE

ANIMAL
Grizzly bear (species also known by many other names)

SCIENTIFIC NAME
Ursus arctos (formerly Ursus horribilis)

DISTRIBUTION
Scattered areas of Europe, northern and central Asia, and northern and western North America

SIZE OF MOTHER
Length of head and body 5-8 feet; weight 200-450 pounds

LENGTH OF PREGNANCY
30-37 weeks

NUMBER OF BABIES
2-3, sometimes 1 or 4

SIZE AT BIRTH
Length 8 inches; weight about 1 pound

EARLY DEVELOPMENT
Newborn have eyes closed, no teeth or fur; stay in den for 3 months

WHEN INDEPENDENT
1½-3 years

WHEN ABLE TO BREED
4-10 years, depending on food supply

and tubers, insects and grubs, small rodents such as mice, fish, elk and caribou calves, and the occasional farm animal. In the fall, the female feeds hungrily and puts on a large amount of body fat. This is her food store for the winter, which she spends in her den.

Born to a dozing mother

The mother's den may be in a rock cave, in a hollow tree, under tree roots, or in an earthen hole the mother has dug herself. She sleeps there for most of the winter, but she does not truly hibernate. In the coldest weather, the body temperature of a real hibernator falls to only a few degrees above freezing. The female grizzly's body temperature drops by only several degrees from normal, to between 70° and 85°F. In mild weather, the bear may rouse herself and leave the den for a short feed.

In the depths of winter, the dozing mother gives birth to tiny, naked cubs, which she licks vigorously. The cubs are so small and unbearlike that ancient people believed she formed their body shape by licking them. In reality, she is only cleaning away the birth fluids, like any other mammal mother. But the belief gave us the saying "to lick into shape."

By about three months of age, the bear cubs have grown tremendously on their mother's milk. Their white-tipped fur is appearing, which gives this type of brown bear the name "grizzly." They are strong enough to leave the den, explore, and follow their mother on feeding trips.

Above *On a family fishing trip, a grizzly cub attempts to swat and scoop fish while keeping its footing in the lake.*

At two or three years of age, the cubs leave their mother and try to find territories of their own. This is a risky time, and some young bears are killed by large males, as they try to establish a territory.

Grizzlies were once widespread, but are no longer so. Fear of their unpredictable tempers, and the need to protect farm animals, led people to trap and shoot them. The grizzly population today is a tiny remnant of the thousands of bears that once roamed most of North America.

Many colors and sizes

Today, most scientists think that the grizzly belongs to the same species, *Ursus arctos*, as many other brown bears around the world. These include the Alaska brown bear, Kodiak bear, Kenai bear, European bear, Russian bear, Asiatic brown bear, Syrian bear, Mexican brown bear, and blue or Himalayan snow bear. Some of these bears were once thought to be separate species. This was due mainly to the huge variation in size and fur color across the animal's range. The Kodiak and Russian brown bears are the biggest, with large males weighing over 1,500 pounds and towering 8 feet tall. The smallest, like the Syrian bears, weigh less than 200 pounds.

BARN OWL

Baby barn owls grow and shed two coats of down, the first one white and the second creamy, before they begin to develop their flight feathers.

Barn owls prospered from the spread of people around the world. The expansion of open fields for farmland, where mice and voles eat the corn and barley, provided barn owls with rich hunting grounds. Their natural nesting sites are holes in trees, rock overhangs, and small caves. But barns, churches, and outbuildings are excellent alternatives.

Barn owls are birds of habit. They hunt through the dusk and night, patrolling a regular route about 15 to 20 feet above the ground with slow, deliberate wingbeats. As they swoop silently along, they watch with their enormous eyes for the slightest movement and listen with their amazingly sensitive ears for rustles in the leaves and grass. Caught in an automobile's headlights, their white underparts and pale brown upper feathers show a ghostly glow.

These birds' regular habits extend to breeding.

Above *The disk of face feathers is developing at 36 days old.*

BABY FACTFILE

ANIMAL
Barn owl

SCIENTIFIC NAME
Tyto alba

DISTRIBUTION
Much of the world except for the far north and parts of Africa, Asia, and Pacific islands; perhaps the most widely distributed of all land birds

SIZE OF MOTHER
Length 14 inches from head to tail

LENGTH OF INCUBATION
4-5 weeks

NUMBER OF BABIES
Average 4-7 eggs

SIZE AT BIRTH
Height 4-5 inches

EARLY DEVELOPMENT
Chicks are blind and helpless at birth, but soon grow down feathers and beg loudly for food

WHEN INDEPENDENT
3-4 months

WHEN ABLE TO BREED
2-3 years

Left *Owlets in their nest.*

The male and female often return to the same site year after year. They make no proper nest, the mother laying her clutch of eggs on a pile of pellets. These owl pellets are the dry remains of mice, beetles, small birds, frogs, and similar creatures. The owl cannot digest the bones, fur, claws, and other hard parts of its food. So it coughs them up, or regurgitates them, as pellets at regular resting sites called roosts.

Roosts can be almost anywhere, from a hollow tree to the roof space of an old house, a bell tower to a church steeple. Most barn owls breed in spring, but in some regions they can raise a family at almost any time of year.

Hatching one by one

The mother owl lays 3 to 12 white eggs in all, but she spaces them out. She lays one egg, then a second a day or two later, and so on. She sits on the increasing clutch to incubate them, or keep them warm, while the father brings her meals.

Each baby owl hatches about 33 days after its egg was laid. This staggered pattern of hatching probably helps the parents to cope with the work load.

The new babies are born with their eyes closed and are covered in sparse down. Soon, they grow their first set of soft, white down feathers. About 12 days later, another set of down feathers appears, which is slightly thicker and creamy in color.

Both mother and father feed their family. They

Above *The young owls gather at feeding time, and the parent passes food to them.*

catch mice, voles, and other prey, and tear these up for the babies. If a predator comes near, the mother barn owl defends her eggs or chicks by spreading her wings over them, hissing, and clacking her beak loudly. The chicks make a variety of noises, from squeaks to snores, and they also snap their beaks fiercely at intruders.

Fledglings in the nest

After about eight weeks, the chicks have grown their adult flight feathers. They practice flapping in the nest. Soon they are ready to take off from the entrance on their first nervous flights into the warm summer night.

By midsummer, the fledglings are learning to hunt for themselves. The parents may continue to bring tidbits almost into the fall. However, the youngsters must leave and establish their own territories.

In recent times, barn owls have run into problems. There are fewer hollow trees and quiet barns in the countryside, their preferred habitat for roosts. Pesticides sprayed onto crops are eaten by small animals that, in turn, are eaten by barn owls. The chemicals may affect the owls' bodies, so that they cannot lay eggs or the eggs fail to hatch. These threats mean that, sadly, the barn owl's eerie night screech and ghostly flight are becoming rarer in many areas.

KOALA

Like other marsupials, the baby koala is born at a very early stage. Its limbs have hardly begun to develop as it wriggles to its mother's pouch.

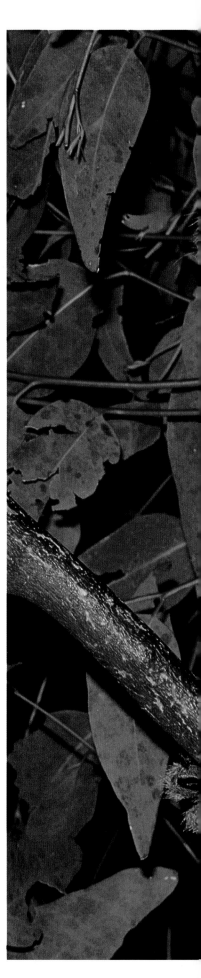

The most amazing feature of a newborn koala is its small size. It is only about the size of a baked bean. It has no fur, and its arms and legs, not yet fully formed, look like flaps of pink rubber. This tiny scrap of life lives in its mother's pouch. Feeding on her rich milk, it grows and develops at a great rate.

By six months of age, the young koala has a luxurious coat of soft gray-brown fur and the typical koala's black snub nose, beady eyes, and tufty ears. It is able to crawl from the pouch and ride on its mother's back.

BABY FACTFILE

ANIMAL
Koala

SCIENTIFIC NAME
Phascolarctos cinereus

DISTRIBUTION
Dry forests of eastern Australia

SIZE OF MOTHER
Height 2 feet; weight 12-18 pounds

LENGTH OF PREGNANCY
4-5 weeks

NUMBER OF BABIES
1

SIZE AT BIRTH
Length ¾ inch; weight ¹/₅₀th ounce

EARLY DEVELOPMENT
The tiny baby lives in its mother's pouch for 5-6 months, suckling milk, then rides on her back

WHEN INDEPENDENT
About 1 year

WHEN ABLE TO BREED
At 2-3 years, but males usually wait another 1-2 years until they are large enough to win females

Above *A young koala with the typical squinting expression.*

Right *The mother koala cuddles her baby protectively.*

Right Mother and baby show why the koala has the nickname "Australia's teddy bear."

Opposite The young koala takes up its regular position on the mother's back.

Although it is sometimes called a "koala bear," the koala is not a true bear. Its young develops in such an extraordinary way because it is a marsupial, or pouched mammal. Other marsupials include the kangaroos and wallabies, and the possums and wombats.

A mother marsupial has a pocket or pouch of skin, called the marsupium, on her chest or belly. The baby leaves her womb and is born at a very early stage in its development. Before its fur has grown, or its paws and feet have fully formed, it crawls through the mother's fur to her pouch. The rest of its development happens while the baby is lying safely in the pouch, feeding on the mother's milk.

The koala's story starts when its mother and father get together in spring. The father's territory overlaps with several females, and he travels around at night, calling to them and mating with them. He also makes noises to chase away other males. The male koala can produce an amazingly strong, growling bellow, which seems much too loud and fierce for such a cuddly looking animal. Koalas also make a grating noise, like the sawing of wood.

Taking it easy

Koalas have a slow, lazy life. They sleep by day in trees, curled up in the forks of branches. At night they eat leaves, nearly always those of eucalyptus, or gum, trees. When a koala needs to move on, it descends to the ground and shuffles along to the next suitable tree. It climbs the trunk with a series of short jumps, digging with its sharp claws into the bark.

The baby koala is usually born around midsummer. It crawls through its mother's fur to the pouch. This opens backward, toward her feet, unlike the forward-opening pouch of the kangaroo. The baby stays there, drinking milk and growing, for several months.

By about six months of age, the baby comes out of the pouch for periods of time. By seven months, the young koala has left the pouch for good. It rides on its mother for the next few months, as it learns to clamber about and grip the bark and branches.

During this time the youngster is also feeding less on milk and more on solid food. Its first food is a mushy pap of half-digested leaves that have already been eaten by the mother – and have passed from her anus. The pap is rich in nutrients and microbes, which enable the young to digest eucalyptus leaves.

By the age of one year, the koala is almost fully grown. It leaves its mother, but it may live nearby for a time. The young koala spends up to 18 hours each day asleep. And it hardly ever drinks – it gets all the moisture it needs from its leafy eucalyptus food.

Saved from extinction

Early settlers in Australia shot millions of koalas, mainly for their fur. By about 1920 this cuddly animal seemed to be heading for extinction. But wildlife authorities protected it and set up nature reserves. Now there are plenty of koalas. Though they live wild only in Australia, they are regular guests at zoos around the world. In the fall, mothers with small babies are a great tourist attraction.

EASTERN COTTONTAIL

Perhaps the behavior of cottontails inspired the old saying "breed like rabbits." This is necessary because so many predators are ready to eat them.

A farmer who sees a new family of baby rabbits might be forgiven for sighing wearily, instead of saying "Aaah!". In many areas, rabbits are pests. They eat farm crops and undermine banks.

The eastern cottontail is far from the greatest digger of the rabbit world. Like its close cousin, the hare, it tends to rest on the surface in a shallow dip or hollow called a form. Or the cottontail may use an abandoned burrow, dug by some other creature.

Breeding like rabbits

The rabbit's ability to reproduce is legendary. Eastern cottontails can begin breeding in February and do not finish until September. This gives them a reproductive season of 8 months, and in a good year, it may be 10 or 11 months.

During a good, long breeding season, a mother may have as many as five litters, or sets, of babies. She may have up to eight babies, or fawns, in each litter, giving her up to 40 offspring in one year. And her daughters are ready to mate and have young only three months after birth. So you can see how the numbers of rabbits could skyrocket!

In most places, though, rabbits never reach their full breeding potential. This is because there are natural checks on the population. The checks include lack of food, harsh conditions such as drought or flood or very cold weather, and predators. Rabbits fall victim to all kinds of hunting animals, from mountain lions and bobcats to coyotes, foxes, snakes, hawks, owls, and humans.

Below *The young cottontail, watching warily, has a large head and short ears compared to the adult.*

BABY FACTFILE

ANIMAL
Eastern cottontail

SCIENTIFIC NAME
Sylvilagus floridanus

DISTRIBUTION
Open country and scattered woodland of eastern United States, from southern Canada down to Central America and extreme northern South America

SIZE OF MOTHER
Length of head and body 12-15 inches; weight 2-4 pounds

LENGTH OF PREGNANCY
4 weeks

NUMBER OF BABIES
Up to 8 in a litter, up to 5 litters a year

SIZE AT BIRTH
Length about 1 inch; weight 1 ounce

EARLY DEVELOPMENT
Born furless and with eyes closed; ready to leave nest at 2 weeks

WHEN INDEPENDENT
3-4 weeks

WHEN ABLE TO BREED
3-5 months

Left Baby cottontail rabbits sit quietly in their nest, called a form. It is above ground, unlike the underground breeding burrows dug by most other types of rabbits.

Adult cottontails lead mainly solitary lives, though they come together to feed and mate during the breeding season. The males, or bucks, fight each other for the right to mate with the females, or does. When a buck and doe pair up, they perform a leaping courtship dance. After mating, the doe drives away the buck.

Fast life cycle

The whole life cycle of the rabbit takes place in the fast lane. The length of an animal's pregnancy is generally linked to its body weight. The female rabbit is pregnant for an average of only four weeks, which is a relatively short time for her size.

The female gives birth in a hollow or scrape in the ground, sheltered in the undergrowth. She has lined the scrape with grasses and mosses, and with soft fur plucked from her own chest. To feed her babies, she stands over them. Her milk is so rich that she need spend only a few minutes each day suckling. Then she covers the babies with camouflaging grass and leaves, and goes off to feed herself.

At birth, the fawns have no fur and their eyelids are closed, but they develop very rapidly. After a week, their fur is growing, and a day or two later their eyes open. By two weeks old, they are ready to leave the nest. At three weeks, they are weaned from their mother's milk and begin to nibble grasses, shoots, and other plant material.

Cottontails are active mainly during dawn and dusk, and at night. Like other rabbits, they eat their own droppings first time around. This helps them get the maximum nutrition from their tough plant foods.

Within a month of birth, the young cottontails are fending for themselves. Their greatest defense is speed. Rabbits have long, powerful back legs for sprinting and leaping. When danger looms, they can bolt away at up to 25 miles per hour. A fleeing rabbit usually follows one of its well-worn tracks and then hides in undergrowth, camouflaged by its neutral brownish coloring. Only the underside of the tail is white – giving the cottontail its name.

RED FOX

When red fox pups first emerge from their den, at about three weeks of age, they may see a remote wilderness – or city buildings.

There are many stories about the fox. It is said to be sly and cunning. It is supposed to kill for pleasure, to raid trash cans, and to steal from chicken coops. Most of these tales are at least partly true. The fox is a clever, agile survivor.

People have hunted and killed red foxes through the ages. Yet the foxes have survived in many areas and have even increased their numbers.

One of the red fox's great advantages is that it is so adaptable. It can live in almost any habitat, from the cold tundra of the far north to warm woodlands and dry scrub. These foxes have spread into cities and suburbs, feeding on the leftover food and scraps we throw away. The urban fox, on patrol in a city street, is a familiar nighttime sight in an automobile's headlights.

The mother fox, known as a vixen, and her mate, the dog fox, court and mate in late winter. People living near fox dens may hear a loud, unearthly, ghostlike howl at night. This is the vixen calling to her mate. Another courting call is a series of short barks or yips.

BABY FACTFILE

ANIMAL
Red fox, also known as silver or cross fox, depending on fur color

SCIENTIFIC NAME
Vulpes vulpes

DISTRIBUTION
North America, Europe, North Africa, and Asia; introduced into Australia

SIZE OF MOTHER
Length of body about 2 feet, tail 12-18 inches; weight 10-13 pounds

LENGTH OF PREGNANCY
7-9 weeks

NUMBER OF BABIES
4-5 pups

SIZE AT BIRTH
Length of body 4-6 inches

EARLY DEVELOPMENT
Pups are born with their eyes closed and brown fur; open eyes at 10-14 days; emerge from den by about 3 weeks

WHEN INDEPENDENT
7-9 months

WHEN ABLE TO BREED
1-2 years

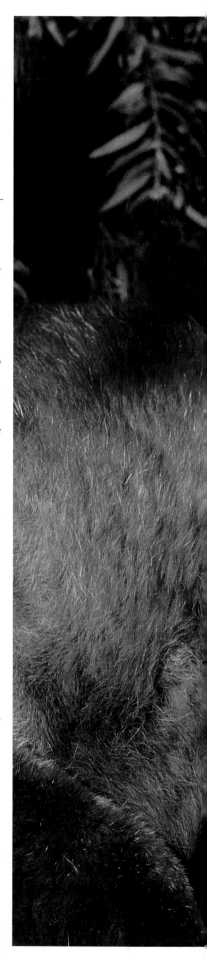

Left *Two fox pups, just two months old, peer out from their underground den.*

Right *These dark-furred pups, lazing on their mother, are about two weeks old.*

Above *The mother fox, or vixen (on the right), has become exasperated by her older pup's play-fighting. She turns and bares her teeth in warning, and the pup crouches in submission.*

Opposite *At six weeks of age, the fox pup has developed its reddish brown fur. But its face is still comparatively rounded and short-muzzled.*

The vixen usually gives birth around March. For fox pups, life begins on the bare soil of their underground den. The den is usually a burrow under tree roots or a rock, or in a rocky crevice. It may have once been a rabbit hole, made larger by the vixen.

The newborn pups, not much bigger than your hand, have their eyes closed. They have tubby round faces and small ears, and they are covered with short chocolate brown fur. Like all newborn mammals, they feed on their mother's milk.

Pretend hunting

There are usually four or five pups in each litter. The mother stays in the den with them at first, and the father brings her food. The pups grow fast, and by two weeks, their blue eyes have opened. Over the next two weeks they begin to take solid food. This is usually eaten and half-digested by the mother, who then coughs it up, or regurgitates it, for her babies.

Gradually the vixen spends more time outside the home. From about three weeks of age, the pups follow her. By a month old, their brown baby fur is being replaced by the familiar reddish brown color with white underparts and tail tip. Their blue eyes turn yellow-amber.

The pups roll and tumble, leap and pounce as they play near the den's entrance. Sometimes they stand up on their back legs and try to "box" with their front paws or nip with their growing teeth. This play fighting is very important. The pups are developing the hunting skills that they will need to survive.

Moving home

Sometimes the mother is disturbed by people or other large animals. Then she may pick up the pups one by one, by the scruff of the neck, and move them to a spare burrow. The pups hang limp and silent in her mouth. Instinct tells them to keep quiet and not struggle.

The fox family stays together through the summer. The mother does most of the pup care and feeding, but the father sometimes helps. During the summer nights, the pups learn to hunt mice, beetles, voles, and worms. They move on to rabbits, small birds, and lizards. They also eat fish and crabs along the shore. In fact, a fox will eat just about anything. Many feast on blackberries and other fruits in the fall.

By the fall, the pups have reached their adult size. Young males usually wander off to live by themselves, but a female may stay with the family group and even help her mother to rear next year's batch of pups. The first fall is a risky time for the youngsters, and many are killed on the roads by vehicles.

WILD BOAR

Like their close cousins, the domestic piglets, young wild boar forage enthusiastically for roots, fruits, and other forest tidbits.

Even people who dislike pigs are usually drawn to the babies of the wild boar. The wide-eyed boarlets have snub snouts, big heads, small bodies, and a furry pattern of dark and light stripes.

Wild boars, often called wild pigs or wild hogs, are the ancient ancestors of the domestic pigs or hogs reared on farms across the world. There are many similarities between them, but the wild boars have kept their natural ways. They are strong, muscular animals, able to live in many different habitats, from thick woodland to open scrub, bush, and grassland.

Wild boars can also eat a huge range of foods. Their taste in plants ranges from acorns and nuts to fruits, roots, buds, leaves, and ferns, and also fungi. In addition, they will take insects, worms, lizards, small birds and their eggs, small mammals such as mice and voles, baby rabbits and hares, and even deer fawns. They may raid farm crops and become pests to the farmers.

Above *These boarlets are as greedy as their domestic counterparts, the piglets, as they crowd together to drink milk from their mother.*

BABY FACTFILE

ANIMAL
Wild boar

SCIENTIFIC NAME
Sus scrofa

DISTRIBUTION
Europe, North Africa, Asia, and Far East; introduced into North America and Australia

SIZE OF MOTHER
Length of head and body 3-4 feet; weight 100-200 pounds

LENGTH OF PREGNANCY
16-17 weeks

NUMBER OF BABIES
About 10

SIZE AT BIRTH
Length about 6-10 inches; weight up to 2 pounds

EARLY DEVELOPMENT
Striped young are born well developed and stay in nest for 10-14 days, then follow mother

WHEN INDEPENDENT
Weaned at 3 months, but stay with mother for up to 2 years

WHEN ABLE TO BREED
18-20 months, but young males cannot usually challenge older males until 3-4 years of age

Left *The young boarlets learn to uncover tasty fungi and tubers.*

The usual family group for wild boars is a small herd called a sounder. It consists of one or a few adult females, the sows, and their babies and youngsters. The males, known as boars, tend to live alone or in small male-only groups.

The boarlets are born in a grass-lined nest in a sheltered place, usually deep in the woodland under-growth. In the northern parts of their range, the sows usually farrow, or give birth, in spring or summer. In tropical areas, they can breed at any time of year.

The babies form a squeaking mound as the mother lies on her side. In this position, the babies can get at her teats, or nipples, to drink her milk. There are 12 teats, and each baby has its own. If there are more than 12 babies, the extra ones usually starve.

The wild boarlets stay in the nest for about 10 to 14 days. At night, their mother goes off to forage and feed. By day, she sleeps with them in the nest, and they suckle her milk.

The babies' striped fur provides good camouflage

Above Dappled sunlight on dead leaves demonstrates the effectiveness of the youngsters' camouflage.

among the shadows of the grasses and bushes. Also, the babies know by instinct to stay very quiet and still. So other animals usually wander past without noticing them.

Learning to forage

After two or three weeks, the wild boar family may leave the nest together for short journeys. By three months of age, the stripes have gone and the young wild boars are growing a coat of stiff, grayish brown hairs. They are also developing their tusks. These oversized teeth are excellent defensive weapons and are good shovels for digging up food.

The young stay with their mother for a year or two, as they grub about for food. They learn how to unearth nuts and roots, forage fruits and bulbs, and catch the occasional small animal.

VIRGINIA OPOSSUM

For baby Virginia opossums, the struggle for survival starts a few minutes after birth. The mother has only 13 teats, yet she may produce up to 50 babies.

To some people, the mother opossum is cute and cuddly, a caring creature who gives her tiny babies piggyback rides. To others, the opossum is nothing more than a big rat, a malodorous pest who steals kitchen scraps, feeds around trash dumps, and occasionally raids henhouses.

Whatever your view, the opossum is a fascinating creature with an unusual method of breeding. Like kangaroos and koalas, it is a marsupial, or pouched mammal. The mother gives birth to her young when they are only the size of your little finger's tip. They have no fur, their eyes are closed, and their bodies, arms, and legs are not yet fully developed.

The main growth and development of opossum babies takes place while they are inside the pouch, a pocketlike flap of skin on the mother's underside. After birth, they crawl through her fur to the pouch. Each one attaches its mouth to one of the teats, or nipples, and immediately begins to feed on its mother's milk.

Another amazing feature of the opossum is the number of babies. There are often around 10 to 20, but up to 50 may emerge at birth! However, the mother has only about 13 teats. So a high percentage of these tiny babies die of starvation soon after they are born.

Below Baby opossums cling uneasily to a dead branch as they practice climbing.

BABY FACTFILE

ANIMAL
Virginia opossum, common opossum, possum

SCIENTIFIC NAME
Didelphis virginiana

DISTRIBUTION
North and Central America

SIZE OF MOTHER
Length of body 12-18 inches

LENGTH OF PREGNANCY
About 2 weeks

NUMBER OF BABIES
More than 40 may be born, but only about 5-10 survive

SIZE AT BIRTH
Length ½ inch; weight less than ¹/₄₀th ounce

EARLY DEVELOPMENT
Tiny opossums crawl into pouch and attach to nipple, stay there for 70 days feeding on milk, then begin to emerge

WHEN INDEPENDENT
4-5 months

WHEN ABLE TO BREED
6-10 months

Above *Eight-week-old youngsters clamber over their mother in typical fashion.*

The surviving babies grow steadily in the pouch. After a few weeks they are able to move about in their warm home, and their fur is growing. By ten weeks of age, they start leaving the pouch and crawling around.

Exploring by night

Usually the mother and her babies sleep by day, huddled together in their nest. This is made of leaves, grass, and other bits of vegetation, sited in a hollow tree, under brush, or in a burrow. The babies still drink her milk. At night, they rest in the nest while the mother goes off to feed.

Over the next week or two, the babies grow big and strong enough to follow their mother on feeding forays. Opossums stay mainly on the ground, but they are good climbers, too. The youngsters can hang from a bough using the grasping, prehensile tail. As they get older and heavier, this feat becomes more difficult.

Sampling food

The young opossums try a wide variety of foods and learn by trial and error what tastes good – and what does not. Insects, such as grasshoppers and beetles, and worms and snails, are some of their early meals. As they grow more skilled at hunting they can catch small birds, voles and mice, snakes and lizards, and even frogs and toads. During the fall and winter, they turn to plant food, such as pokeberries and persimmon. By six months of age, the youngsters are just about fully grown. They leave their mother for life on their own.

WHITE-TAILED DEER

A baby white-tailed deer's instincts are so strong that it stays completely still and silent, even when predators (and people) pass a few yards away.

BABY FACTFILE

ANIMAL
White-tailed deer, Virginia deer

SCIENTIFIC NAME
Odocoileus virginianus

DISTRIBUTION
North and Central America, down to middle of South America; introduced into places such as New Zealand and Scandinavia

SIZE OF MOTHER
Height 3 feet at shoulder; length 4-5 feet; weight 100-150 pounds

LENGTH OF PREGNANCY
29 weeks

NUMBER OF BABIES
1 for new mother, 2 or 3 in later years

SIZE AT BIRTH
Height 10-12 inches at shoulder

EARLY DEVELOPMENT
Babies can walk within minutes of birth; hide in undergrowth for the first few weeks

WHEN INDEPENDENT
4-5 months

WHEN ABLE TO BREED
Females at 1-2 years, males at 2-3 years, depending on success in the rut

White-tailed deer are one of the most common "game," or hunted, animals in North America. However, the baby, or fawn, is rarely seen. It hides in the bushes and dense undergrowth, without the slightest movement. Instinctively it remains silent. The fawn's light-spotted brown coat provides excellent camouflage, making it blend with the dappled shade among the leaves, twigs, and stems.

Predators and people may pass near the location, unaware of the youngster hiding in the shadows. The mother deer, or doe, may be waiting nearby. When all is clear, she returns quietly to her baby, and the fawn hungrily drinks her milk.

If a predator pauses and begins to sniff around near the fawn, the mother deer may fend off the predator or distract it. She makes herself known by moving in the undergrowth to divert and draw away the predator.

Right *A mother deer washes the rear end of her two-week-old fawn as it sniffs curiously at the ground.*

Opposite *This fawn was photographed in June, curled up in one of its resting places.*

Unlike many other deer, which live in large herds, white-tailed deer are often solitary or join small family groups. During the winter they may band together to survive. They forage for food and keep watch for predators.

In the winter the males, or bucks, display their antlers and strength. They have terrific shoving matches and antler-wrestling battles with rivals. This period is called the rut, and during it the bucks fight for the right to mate with the females.

In early to midsummer the does retire into dense undergrowth and give birth to their fawns. These are born fully furred, with creamy light spots on their midbrown coats. The new fawns can stand and walk, in a wobbly fashion, within minutes of birth.

Avoiding danger

The fawn stays hidden in the undergrowth for the first few weeks, camouflaged by its spotted coat. The mother returns five or six times each day to feed the baby on her rich milk. She communicates with her young by a soft bleat or a warning bark.

After a week or two, the fawn begins to nibble at the vegetation. It tries various plants and learns to identify the softer, tastier ones. Gradually the youngster spends more time feeding in the open. This is one of the riskiest times for the young deer. Instinctively, it looks up regularly while feeding. A deer lives on its senses, and it relies on sharp hearing, smell, and eyesight to detect the slightest hint of danger. Bobcats, mountain lions, coyotes, and bears prey upon fawns as well as adult deer. The deer are also hunted by golden eagles and other large raptors (birds of prey).

By four months of age, the fawn is no longer taking its mother's milk, and it is eating leaves, twigs, and grasses. Its spotted coat is replaced by the adult winter fur, which is longer and grayer. Young does may stay with their mother for a year or more, but the bucks usually leave before they are a year old.

Fall and rise

When European settlers arrived in North America, white-tailed deer were found in many areas of the continent. So was its close western relative, the mule deer. The early settlers hunted deer because their flesh was tasty and their hides could be made into durable leather clothing called "buckskins."

Right *The dappling on the coat of this white-tailed deer fawn blends in with the daisies and other flowers in a midsummer meadow. The white underside of the tail gives this deer its name.*

The number of white-tailed deer declined, and at one time this species was endangered. But laws were introduced; and the deer began to recover their numbers.

Currently, many areas of the United States are experiencing a deer population explosion. Residential communities, farmland, and the timber industry have all changed the face of the landscape to partially cleared forests, increasing the areas of scattered woodlands, clearings, and open bushland that are the deer's preferred habitat. In addition, predators such as wolves, mountain lions, and bears once occupied the same habitats as the white-tailed deer. These large carnivores effectively kept a check on the deer population, naturally culling the old, the infirm, and the young. Wolves, mountain lions, and bears have been eradicated from most of the white-tailed deer's range and are no longer considered to be major predators.

Above This newborn fawn is only nine minutes old, yet it has already been partly washed by its mother, and is now nuzzling her and feeding on her milk.

When managed hunting seasons were again resumed, game regulators allowed hunters to take only one buck per season. Does were protected throughout the year.

Today, even though hunting seasons are strictly controlled, deer continue to thrive on public and private lands, which cannot provide enough space and food. The deer venture into suburban residential areas and farmlands. They are considered pests by some and help to spread an illness called Lyme's disease. Although their natural predators are now much less numerous, each year thousands of deer are injured or killed as they attempt to cross the roadways. As a consequence, automobiles are considered a significant "predator."

WOOD MOUSE

*The wood mouse is an exceptionally
widespread mammal. It lives not only in
woods, but also in grassland, farmland,
hillsides, parks, and gardens.*

We measure our lives in months and years. The wood mouse's life is measured in hours and days. This tiny mammal, a member of the rodent group, has a childhood lasting only three weeks.

Survival is a difficult task for such a small creature. The wood mouse ventures out mainly at night, using its whiskers to feel its way through the darkness. It has good sight and hearing, and an excellent sense of smell. However, the wood mouse is relatively defenseless, and many fall prey to owls, hawks, crows, cats, weasels, foxes, and other predators.

The mouse's main survival strategy is to breed at speed. A single mother may have several litters, or sets, of babies, totaling 25 to 30 offspring in a year. With so many babies, the chances are that only one or two will survive.

The wood mouse has many similarities to its close cousin, the house mouse. For both, life starts in a cozy nest. Wood mice build their nests underground and line them with grass, straw, and leaves, shredded by the mother. The new babies, known as pups, are pink and furless. Their eyes are closed, and there is no sign of the typically large mouse ears. They depend completely on their mother. She suckles them with her milk, licks them clean, removes their droppings, and keeps the nest clean. If they wriggle too far, she picks them up in her mouth and returns them to the nest.

BABY FACTFILE

ANIMAL
Wood mouse

SCIENTIFIC NAME
Apodemus sylvaticus

DISTRIBUTION
*Woodlands and fields of Europe,
North Africa, and Asia*

SIZE OF MOTHER
*Length of head and body 3-4
inches, tail about the same; weight
³/₅th ounce*

LENGTH OF PREGNANCY/INCUBATION
25-26 days

NUMBER OF BABIES
*About 6 in a litter, up to 5 litters a
year*

SIZE AT BIRTH
Length ½ inch

EARLY DEVELOPMENT
*Born furless and helpless with
eyes closed; leave nest at 16 days*

WHEN INDEPENDENT
21 days

WHEN ABLE TO BREED
2 months

*Below In this view from
above, the mother mouse
and her babies, which are
about ten days old, sleep
in a tangled heap in their
nest.*

By about five days old the baby mice are growing their fur. At ten days, their eyes are open, and their limbs are bigger and stronger. Their movements are coordinated enough for the youngsters to crawl some way from the nest. Little more than two weeks after birth, the young mice venture from the nest and crawl along the burrow, up to the surface.

Family life

Wood mice dig extensive burrows among tree roots and in leaf litter. They rest by day in the burrows and store food there in times of plenty. The mice usually live in pairs or family groups, which range over an area about half the size of a football field. Although

Above *A revealing cutaway of the wood mice's burrow entrance, tunnel, underground nest, and food store.*

they are named "wood" mice, these creatures dwell in many other habitats, including sand dunes, farmland, gardens, and even hillsides and moorland.

At about three weeks of age, the young mice are making the transition from mother's milk to solid foods. They eat seeds, nuts, fruits, berries, buds, shoots, and fungi, as well as insects, grubs, snails, and worms. Ever cautious, a feeding wood mouse pauses regularly to look, listen, and sniff. If disturbed, it can leap more than 3 feet through the air and then bound away on its large back feet.

TROPICAL FORESTS

Tropical forests are the richest habitats in the world, home to a wealth of plants and animals. On some days, the sun shines brightly. At other times, a cloudburst soaks the terrain. The continual warmth, light, and moisture encourage the riot of tree and flower growth that makes a tropical forest. With such a huge range of growing food, herbivores are both numerous and diverse – many having specialized to feed on particular plants. And with such a huge range of prey to eat, the carnivores are varied, too. Indeed, tropical forest creatures belong to one of the most complex food webs on Earth.

Right *Tigers are fond of watery places. Here, a mother and her partly grown cub pause among long grass and reeds to drink from a pool.*

Opposite *Tiger cubs give their wide-eyed, all-inquisitive stare. Note that their markings are slightly different. Each set of markings is as unique as our fingerprints.*

Below *Map showing the distribution of the tropical forests and the featured animal species.*

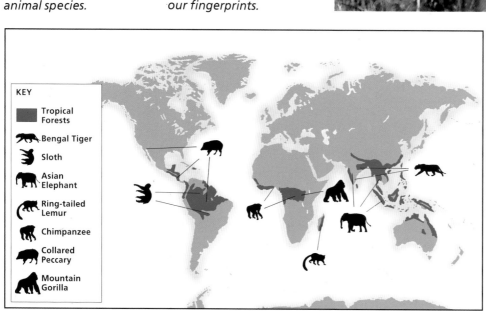

KEY

Tropical Forests

Bengal Tiger

Sloth

Asian Elephant

Ring-tailed Lemur

Chimpanzee

Collared Peccary

Mountain Gorilla

BENGAL TIGER

As fluffy tiger cubs play rough and tumble, they are learning the hunting techniques that will enable them to become "lords of the jungle."

More than 20 years ago, a baby tiger was in great danger of becoming an orphan. Today, the risk is much smaller. Tigers are among the world's largest and most endangered carnivorous mammals. These magnificent big cats once roamed widely across India. Sadly, thousands were shot as trophies by big-game hunters and royalty. Often these tigers were mothers, with cubs hidden nearby. The mother would come into the open to defend her offspring against the human hunters on their brightly decorated ceremonial elephants. She was shot and the hunters moved on, leaving the terrified cubs to starve.

Operation Tiger

Thousands of tigers were shot or poisoned to protect farm animals and people. Their wild scrub and forest habitat gradually shrank as deforestation claimed land for farms, factories, houses, and roads.

In 1973, the Indian government launched Operation Tiger to save the Bengal tiger from extinction. Hunting tigers and trading their skins, meat, and body parts were banned. Large areas of land were set aside as nature reserves. Other Asian countries joined the rescue effort. Today, other subspecies of tigers living in Siberia, Arabia, southeast Asia, and eastern China are perilously endangered by loss of habitat and poaching in these regions.

Male and female tigers come together only for a few days to mate. For the rest of their time, these fearsome predators live alone. The female usually gives birth in spring or summer, to about three or four cubs, though sometimes as many as seven.

A tiger cub weighs around 3 pounds. It is as blind and helpless as a newborn pet kitten, with its

Below A tiger female relaxes with her cub. The beautiful, clean, white underfur is usually hidden as the tiger walks and stalks.

BABY FACTFILE

ANIMAL
Bengal tiger, tiger

SCIENTIFIC NAME
Panthera tigris

DISTRIBUTION
Restricted areas of India

SIZE OF MOTHER
Length 9 feet including tail; weight 300-350 pounds

LENGTH OF PREGNANCY
15 weeks

NUMBER OF BABIES
3-4 cubs

SIZE AT BIRTH
Weight 2-3 pounds

EARLY DEVELOPMENT
Blind and helpless at birth; able to follow mother by 8 weeks

WHEN INDEPENDENT
2-3 years

WHEN ABLE TO BREED
3-4 years

Left This five-week-old tiger cub is beginning to lose its kittenish cuddliness and develop the longer muzzle, squarer face, and more angular features of the adult.

parents' striped fur, which provides such good camouflage in undergrowth and long grass.

At first, the mother tiger guards her young in a den among rocks or roots. The cubs feed on her milk, and lie still and quiet while she is away hunting. After two weeks, their eyes open. They continue to suckle her milk for another four weeks. Then she weans them to the diet of a true carnivore – meat.

On their first expeditions from the den, tiger cubs play and sleep in the sunshine, while their mother watches for danger. The cuddly cubs pounce and roll like pet kittens, but this is no idle pastime. Instinctively, the cubs strengthen their muscles and sharpen their senses. They begin to learn hunting skills needed for survival.

This appealing, kittenish stage lasts only a short time. By six months of age, the cubs are about half-grown. They can kill their own prey, such as small monkeys and baby deer. They can also swim well.

Tigers like water and often cool off by lying at the edge of a jungle pool.

The growing offspring watch their mother hunt, learn from her, and share the meat of her larger prey such as antelopes, wild pigs, and full-grown deer. They keep mainly within her range, unless prey or water becomes very scarce.

At the age of two years, the young tigers are almost fully grown. They have perfected the art of stealth, since a tiger kills by ambush. It creeps as near to its chosen prey as possible, then makes a fast charge.

Around this time, the mother stops sharing food with the cubs and may actively chase them away. It is a tough period, because most of the surrounding land is already occupied by adult tigers with established territories. If the young adults stray outside the reserves, they will probably be captured and brought back or shot by poachers.

SLOTH

Life could not be much slower for the sloth, which spends much of its time asleep. Baby sloths even seem to play in slow motion.

Would you like to be a sloth and live life in the slow lane? It might seem easy and lazy, but you would soon be very bored. Sloths do almost nothing except hang upside down in trees all day, eat leaves, and sleep. Even their digestion is slow – they only produce droppings once a week.

There are five kinds, or species, of sloths, all of which lead similar lives. They also look similar to each other, with small faces and straggly fur. They have long, curved, 3-inch claws on their fingers and toes, which work like hooks.

Born in the trees

On the ground, sloths can only drag themselves along awkwardly. But among the branches, they are completely at home. A sloth lives almost all of its sedate life in the trees, eating, resting, sleeping, courting, mating, and even giving birth there.

Baby sloths can be born at nearly any time of year. The mother usually has just one baby, which looks like a miniature version of her. It has long fur, a baby face, and small versions of the long claws. The new arrival hooks itself into its mother's fur. She shows it where her teat is, and the baby sucks its first meal of mother's milk.

The mother sloth carries her baby on her belly. Since she usually hangs upside down, this means the baby is the usual way up. The young sloth's gray-brown fur soon acquires the greenish tinge of an

Left *A baby three-toed sloth peeps from its customary position on the mother's belly as she clings nonchalantly to a tree trunk with her hooked claws.*

BABY FACTFILE

ANIMAL
Sloth

SCIENTIFIC NAMES
5 species including Choloepus didactylus *(common two-toed sloth), and* Bradypus tridactylus *(pale-throated three-toed sloth)*

DISTRIBUTION
Forests of Central and South America

SIZE OF MOTHER
Length of head and body 20-24 inches; weight 8-15 pounds

LENGTH OF PREGNANCY
About 24-28 weeks, up to 50 weeks in some species

NUMBER OF BABIES
1

SIZE AT BIRTH
Length 4-6 inches; weight 10-14 ounces

EARLY DEVELOPMENT
Born in a tree; suckled for about 4 weeks by mother, then gathers leaves and feeds on leaves pre-digested by mother

WHEN INDEPENDENT
9 months

WHEN ABLE TO BREED
3-5 years

adult sloth. This is due to tiny plantlike organisms that grow in the grooves of the coarse hairs. The green color and the sloth's extreme slowness combine to make mother and baby well camouflaged among the greenery of the tropical forest.

The mother sloth eats leaves and needs huge quantities of them to fill her enormous stomach. One-third of a well-fed sloth's body weight may be the leaves in its stomach. They ferment and digest there for weeks.

A few weeks after birth, the growing youngster begins to reach out from its place on the mother's belly and hook leaves toward its mouth, to test-chew them. It also eats leaves that the mother has already chewed, swallowed, and then regurgitated, or brought up again. The predigested, softened leaves are easier for the baby to digest.

Soon the young sloth starts to leave its mother for short periods, and learns to hang and clamber among the branches. It takes milk for about a month, then

Above This young sloth has not yet acquired the green algae-tinged fur of its mother.

feeds solely on mother's predigested leaves and food it gathers itself. If the youngster becomes separated from its mother, it makes whistling and lamblike bleating sounds to attract her attention.

Defensive claws

Adult sloths live alone, and the father takes no part in family life. At about nine months of age, the growing youngster is independent, though it stays in its mother's part of the forest for another year or two. It is able to defend itself against predators, such as jaguars and ocelots, by slashing with the fearsome claws and biting. However, the sloth's best defense is its good camouflage, helped by its lazy lifestyle – just hangin' around.

ASIAN ELEPHANT

Elephants are very family-oriented animals. The infant is protected and cared for by other adult females as well as by its mother.

When a baby elephant is born, it has no shortage of helpers. Elephants are very social animals and live in well-knit family groups called herds. During the birth, the mother, or cow, elephant may be assisted by other females, or "midwives." Upon the baby's arrival, the midwives help the new baby out of the bag, or membranes, that surrounded it in the womb. They stroke it with their trunks and encourage it to stand on its wobbly legs.

If a tiger or other predator sniffs around, the adult females will surround the baby and gather the other youngsters in the herd. Few hunting creatures are desperate enough to take on such huge, powerful, and determined opposition.

BABY FACTFILE

ANIMAL
Asian or Indian elephant

SCIENTIFIC NAME
Elephas maximus

DISTRIBUTION
Indian subcontinent east to the mainland and islands of southeast Asia.

SIZE OF MOTHER
Height 7-9 feet; length of head and body 16-20 feet; weight up to 10,000 pounds

LENGTH OF PREGNANCY
90-96 weeks

NUMBER OF BABIES
Usually 1

SIZE AT BIRTH
Height 3 feet; weight 200-250 pounds

EARLY DEVELOPMENT
Baby can stand and feed on milk minutes after birth; walks with herd at 2 days; grows rapidly

WHEN INDEPENDENT
3-5 years

WHEN ABLE TO BREED
Females at 10 years under favorable conditions; males later when they reach full size and win battles with other males

Left This baby Asian elephant is testing out its trunk on a banana stem.

Right The day after its birth, this baby scratches itself as its huge mother looms above reassuringly.

The regular elephant herd is a group of females with their babies and youngsters. Young adult males, or bulls, may gather in loose bachelor herds. Older males tend to live alone.

The regular herd is led by the senior female, called the matriarch, who may be over 50 years old. The herd roams the forest and bushland, foraging on leaves, grass, and other plant parts, such as fruits, blossoms, twigs, young bark, and soft roots. The experienced matriarch remembers the locations of pools and rivers for drinking and bathing, and how feeding areas change with the seasons. The saying "elephants never forget" has more than a little truth.

A safe hiding place

Within two days, the baby elephant can keep up with the wandering herd. It looks quite hairy in comparison with the adults, which have small, sparse hairs scattered over their thick skin. The baby feeds on its mother's milk, which comes from teats on the paired breasts between her front legs. It does this for up to four years, one of the longest suckling periods of any mammal.

The baby elephant is also tended by other young females known as "aunts" or "allomothers." It learns to communicate with its mother and aunts by touching and sniffing with its trunk, and by making

Above Two adults and a calf search for shade under a tree.

Below Young bull (male) elephants play-fight to test their strength and technique.

low rumbling sounds. If danger threatens, it rushes to its mother or an aunt, and hides between her legs.

Above *A day-old calf feeds from the teat between its mother's front legs.*

Tusk variation

An elephant's tusks are enlarged incisor teeth from the upper jaw. Made of the unique substance dentin, or ivory, they start to grow at two years old. If the young elephant is a male, its tusks will continue to grow throughout life. However, they rarely reach the gigantic size seen in the bulls of the African elephant. The tusks of female Asian elephants seldom grow long enough to show beyond the lips.

At the age of six years, the young elephant weighs ten times as much as it did at birth. By then it is feeding on leaves, grass, and other vegetation. From about ten years onward, the elephant matures and can breed. Females tend to stay with their family group, but males leave to join the bachelor herds.

RING-TAILED LEMUR

The lemur troop has a well-organized lifestyle, with various ways of communicating about food, danger, and social rank.

Lemurs are medium-sized mammals that look like a cross between a cat and a squirrel. There are about 12 types, or species, in the lemur family, all of which live on the large island of Madagascar, to the east of Africa. In the past there were far more lemur species. Then people settled parts of Madagascar, bringing their farm animals and other creatures with them, and many lemurs became extinct.

The word *lemur* means "ghost." Most lemurs seem to live ghostly lives among the shadows of the tropical forests. The ring-tailed lemur is active mainly by day, and prefers to move about and travel on the ground. When it does leap into the trees, using its long, muscular limbs, this fairly large lemur likes to stay on stout branches.

Ring-tailed lemurs dwell in groups. They have a complicated social life, like their cousins, the monkeys and apes. They smear their tails with secretions from their scent glands and wave them at rivals.

Group life

In most smaller species of lemur, the newborn babies are naked and helpless, with their eyelids closed. But the newborn ring-tailed lemur is covered with fur, like its parents, and its eyes are open. The baby clings to the fur on its mother's underside for the first few days and feeds regularly on her milk. Later it is able to hold onto her upper side and ride piggyback.

Ring-tailed lemurs live in mixed groups of up to 30. The group occupies a territory as large as 60 acres. A young lemur must find its place in the ranking system, or dominance hierarchy, within the group. There are hierarchies for both the females and the males.

As the young lemur grows, it begins to eat adult food of fruits, leaves, bark, and sap. By six months of age, the youngster is fully independent. If female, she is likely to stay in the group where she was born. If male, he will probably leave to join another group.

Civets, members of the cat family, may catch a young or sick lemur. When such a ground predator appears, the lemurs utter a series of alarm calls and scuttle into the trees. But, in general, the greatest threat comes from above.

One of the first important events in the young lemur's life will probably be an air raid. When an eagle or hawk is sighted, the lemurs let out a different series of loud calls and scatter into the undergrowth. However, they may be too late. The bird can swoop from behind a hill or tree and snatch a young, inexperienced lemur before it reaches cover.

Above *Young lemurs climb more readily than the adults.*

Opposite *A baby clings to its mother's back, while above, an adult is wrapped in its ringed tail.*

BABY FACTFILE

ANIMAL
Ring-tailed lemur

SCIENTIFIC NAME
Lemur catta

DISTRIBUTION
Scattered forest and scrub of Madagascar

SIZE OF MOTHER
Length of head and body 16-20 inches, tail 20-24 inches; weight 5-8 pounds

LENGTH OF PREGNANCY
19-20 weeks

NUMBER OF BABIES
Usually 1, sometimes 2 or 3

SIZE AT BIRTH
Length 3-4 inches

EARLY DEVELOPMENT
Born well developed, with fur and eyes open

WHEN INDEPENDENT
5-7 months

WHEN ABLE TO BREED
1-2 years

CHIMPANZEE

As baby chimps play, explore, and rest with their mothers, they exhibit many behavior characteristics similar to human babies.

Together with the gorilla, the chimpanzee is our closest cousin in the animal world. Most people feel an immediate kinship with this great ape, with its large range of facial gestures, body postures, and expressive sounds.

The chimp has a skill once attributed only to humans but now known to occur in various animal groups – the use of simple tools. The chimp even makes its own tools for specific purposes. It will take a leafy twig and strip the leaves to make a long, thin stick for use as a termite catcher. The chimp pokes it through a narrow entrance into a termite nest, then it extracts the stick and licks off the juicy termites.

Chimps also crush leaves in their palms for use as sponges. They hold the leaves in water that they cannot reach with their mouths, such as that in a hollow log. Then they extract the waterlogged, leafy sponge and suck the moisture from it.

Long learning period

In captivity, chimps have been taught to use human sign language and "talk" with a sense of understanding and purpose. And they have shown amazing adeptness at solving problems.

Like the young of gorillas and humans, baby chimps have a long childhood, up to ten years in some cases. During this time they find out how to feed and groom themselves, avoid danger, and communicate with other members of their group, called a community or troop. Their behavior is partly instinctive, or inbuilt. They also learn by observing other members of the group, and through trial and error.

The newborn chimp, covered in long, sparse, black fur, is almost totally helpless. It is able to do little except nurse. Even the gripping reflexes, or automatic actions, of its hands and feet are not well developed. So the mother must hold the baby to her. After a few days the baby can cling to her fur and begins to hold onto her belly. By six months of age, it is usually able to ride piggyback.

Above *A mother grooms her baby.*

Right *An older mother with juvenile and baby.*

BABY FACTFILE

ANIMAL
Chimpanzee

SCIENTIFIC NAME
Pan troglodytes

DISTRIBUTION
Forest, woodland, and shrubland of western and central Africa

SIZE OF MOTHER
Height about 4 feet; length of head and body 28-34 inches; weight 60-100 pounds

LENGTH OF PREGNANCY
32-34 weeks

NUMBER OF BABIES
1

SIZE AT BIRTH
Length about 9-12 inches; weight 2-4 pounds

EARLY DEVELOPMENT
Newborn can cling to mother after a few days; crawls after several weeks; rides on mother's back at 5-7 months; weaning starts at 2 years old

WHEN INDEPENDENT
4-8 years

WHEN ABLE TO BREED
Usually after 11-12 years, though courtship patterns develop from 3-4 years

Above A large, mature male stands protectively over a young chimpanzee mother as she cradles her baby.

Opposite Young chimps are intensely curious. They put many objects into their mouths to assess texture and taste, just like human babies.

The baby chimp has a large head relative to its body. This makes it top-heavy, and sitting up and crawling are difficult and tiring at first. However, like human and gorilla babies, it slowly learns to sit, crawl, and then walk.

The chimp mother grooms and plays with her baby. By about two years of age, the baby is suckling less and the mother allows it to take her food. The baby sleeps with its mother at night, in a tree nest of broken and bent-over twigs and boughs, until the age of about three years.

Chimps usually live in large, loose groups of 100 or more individuals. These are made up of smaller parties, of about three to seven chimps. The chimps in a party spend most of the day feeding, socializing, and grooming themselves and each other. Two or three may form long-lasting "friendships." They establish their seniority and rank in the group by a complicated system of facial expressions, postures, and sounds.

For the first few years, a young chimp rarely strays far from its mother. It may climb, play with, and tease other members of its party, and they tolerate it. But the youngster is always ready to rush back to its mother, even at seven or eight years of age.

People who watch chimps in the wild have noticed that mothers vary in the amount of time and care they devote to their offspring. Some mothers almost ignore their babies, while others put so much time and effort into child care that they seem to "spoil" their young.

Although slow to develop in many ways, chimps show courting behavior very early. Males as young as two try to mate with adult females, even though their sexual organs will not be fully formed and functional until years later. From about four years of age, young males and females go through the actions of courting, with adults and with each other.

Females are mature and able to have babies of their own at about 11 to 14 years of age. They may then leave the community where they were born and move to another one. Males rarely do this.

Hunting and raiding

Many years ago, chimps were believed to be peace-loving vegetarians. Since the 1950s, much patient observation of these great apes in the wild has altered this view. Chimps do feed mainly on fruits, young leaves, and insects. But they may form bands to hunt monkeys, wild pigs, and small antelopes. They tear the prey apart with great shrieks and whoops.

Chimps may also show aggression, both within and between communities. Physical fighting is uncommon, and serious injury is less so, but it does happen. In some rain forest areas, a number of male chimps from a community form a small group and patrol the borders of their area. They call to warn off intruding chimps from neighboring areas. If they meet one or two strange chimps, the border patrollers may attack and even kill them.

COLLARED PECCARY

Resembling the true wild pigs, with their stocky bodies and short legs, peccaries are agile, speedy, and well able to evade predators of the forest.

There are three kinds of peccary, all of which are piglike creatures. The one most familiar to us is the collared peccary, named from the "collar" of pale fur around its neck. Its range extends from the southwestern United States down to Argentina. It is an adaptable creature, able to live in various habitats from rain forest to dry scrubland. However, the peccaries as a group are mainly forest dwellers.

Collared peccaries live in herds containing 10 to 50 males, females, and youngsters. The herd consists of several family subgroups. Collared peccaries do not seem to form long-term pairs. Instead, each female may mate with several males and vice versa.

When a female is about to give birth, she leaves the herd and finds a cave, large burrow, or hollow in a hillside. The babies, usually two, are born furred and with eyes open. Almost at once, they are alert and able to stand. They are covered in reddish hair with a dark stripe down the back, which contrasts with the mother's gray-brown grizzled coat and pale collar.

A few hours after birth, the pigletlike babies can walk and run. After two or three days, mother and babies return to the herd. She feeds her youngsters on milk for up to eight weeks. From the age of three weeks, they also begin to nose around for roots, seeds, fruits, berries, and other plant parts. Gradually the youngsters widen their diet to include insects, worms, and other small animals. Collared peccaries have very strong jaws and teeth, and can even eat cacti!

BABY FACTFILE

ANIMAL
Collared peccary

SCIENTIFIC NAME
Tayassu tajacu

DISTRIBUTION
Forests, scrub, and dry brushland of southwestern North America, and Central and South America

SIZE OF MOTHER
Height 16-18 inches at shoulder; length 3 feet; weight 40-50 pounds

LENGTH OF PREGNANCY
20 weeks

NUMBER OF BABIES
1-4, usually 2

SIZE AT BIRTH
Length 8-12 inches

EARLY DEVELOPMENT
Baby has reddish fur with dark back stripe; can run a few hours after birth; eats solid food at 3-4 weeks; weaned at 6-8 weeks

WHEN INDEPENDENT
5-7 months

WHEN ABLE TO BREED
Females at 8-9 months, males at 11-12 months

Below *These recently born babies have huge heads in comparison to their small bodies and limbs. There is only the merest hint of the light "collar" of neck fur.*

The herd feeds mainly during the cooler parts of the day and twilight. During hot periods and in the middle of the night, the peccaries rest in thickets or abandoned burrows.

A protected childhood

Peccaries have poor eyesight, but good senses of smell and hearing. They are constantly on the alert for their two main predators, mountain lions and jaguars. When danger looms, they band together, rasp their teeth, and pretend to charge at the enemy. Any member of the herd will protect the babies, allowing them to hide between its rear legs.

One herd member may rush forward and confront the predator. The defender could be injured or killed while the rest of the herd escapes. Such action is called altruistic behavior.

Above A chubby young collared peccary looks on as its mother sniffs the ground for tasty tubers and roots.

By the age of about one month, the young peccaries are growing their neck collar of pale fur. They still stay close to mother, and should they lose her, they make a shrill, clucking call. When the herd finds a particularly rich source of food, such as a tree that is dropping ripe fruit, the adults stand back and let the young feed first. However, this privileged life only lasts until the youngsters are about six months old and nearly full grown. At this relatively young age, the young peccaries must begin to forage for food and to run with a herd should a predator threaten. The youngsters, as herd members, learn quickly that life offers few privileges.

MOUNTAIN GORILLA

For many years, people believed that gorillas were aggressive and violent. In fact, peaceable gorillas would be justified in leveling those charges against humans.

Mountain gorillas are among the world's rarest animals. Only a few hundred survive in the tropical mountain forests of Zaire, Rwanda, and Uganda, in Africa. They live at heights of 6,000 to 12,000 feet. They are protected by law and by their rising fame as a tourist attraction. Despite this, these magnificent creatures are still killed by poachers.

Gorillas are the largest of the great apes. The gorilla and another ape, the chimpanzee, are our closest cousins in the animal world. When you look at a baby gorilla clinging to its mother, you can see echoes of the relationship between a human baby and its mother.

A gorilla mother may give birth at any time of year. The newborn gorilla is similar to a newborn human in many ways. It does little except feed on its mother's milk, rest, and sleep. Occasionally it waves its arms and legs around, and makes "crying" sounds.

The newborn's gray-pink skin turns jet black after a few days. Its eyes focus and see more clearly in its second week. It begins to crawl by about the ninth week, and can sit up by 12 or 13 weeks old. For most of this time, the baby clings to its mother's fur.

BABY FACTFILE

ANIMAL
Mountain gorilla

SCIENTIFIC NAME
Gorilla gorilla beringei

DISTRIBUTION
Mountain forests of central Africa

SIZE OF MOTHER
Height 5 feet; weight 200 pounds

LENGTH OF PREGNANCY
36-37 weeks

NUMBER OF BABIES
1

SIZE AT BIRTH
Weight 4-5 pounds

EARLY DEVELOPMENT
Born helpless like a human baby, and clings to mother's fur; gray-pink skin darkens after a few days; suckles for 2-3 years

WHEN INDEPENDENT
About 3 years

WHEN ABLE TO BREED
Females at 6-7 years, males at 8-10 years but often later for social reasons

Above *A female gorilla rests pensively with her baby in the deep tropical undergrowth. This scene dispels the belief held by humans only a few decades ago that gorillas are ferocious and bloodthirsty.*

Left *Mother and young son rest on a lichen-covered tree buttress in the high forest of Rwanda in eastern Africa. They clearly show the relatively long fur of the mountain gorilla.*

About six months after birth, the young gorilla learns to walk and climb. It plays with other young-sters in the gorilla group, known as a troop. It also teases the adults. Even the huge mature male, which leads and defends the troop, tolerates the playfulness. This chief male is known as the silverback, because he has silvery fur on his back and sides.

Over the next year, the young gorilla will discover plant foods, though it still relies on mother's milk. Gorillas are entirely vegetarian and will eat leaves, shoots, stems, and roots of plants. Occasionally, they will eat fruit and insects.

The gorilla troop is active mainly during the morning and evening, with a rest around midday. The youngsters and females climb trees, but the large males are usually too heavy. At dusk, the gorillas bend over branches and creepers to make a nest, where they sleep during the night. Almost the only predator that hunts baby gorillas is the leopard.

A young gorilla stays with its mother, feeding on her milk and sleeping in her nest, for up to three years. Then, a young female gorilla is likely to leave and join another troop. A juvenile male may wander alone, becoming stronger and more mature. His silvery back fur usually appears at about ten years old. However, he will not have the power or experi-ence to begin his own troop, or take over an existing one, until about 15 to 20 years of age.

MOUNTAINS

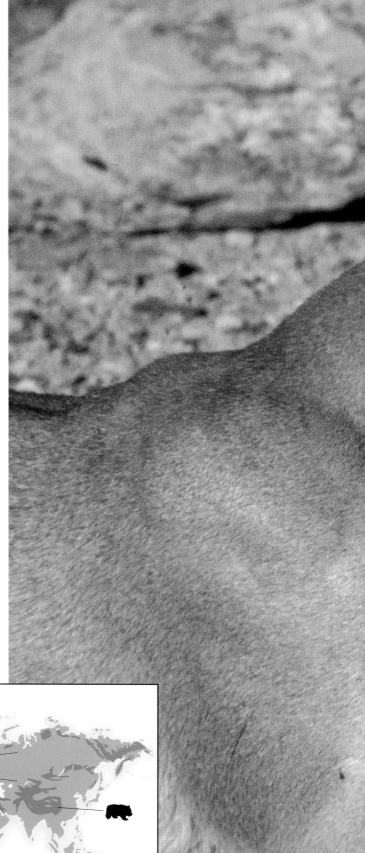

Howling winds, scarce food, and lack of shelter are the main challenges in mountain life. Most of the animals who roam the high slopes are large and mobile, from the agile mountain lions and leaping mountain goats to the freely soaring eagles. Their babies are brought into a world of rocky slopes, small stunted plants, and deep winter snowfalls.

Above *A mountain lion cub practices focusing.*

Right *This young mountain lion is learning how to get at the flesh of a turtle brought back by the mother.*

Below *Map showing the distribution of major mountain areas and the featured animal species.*

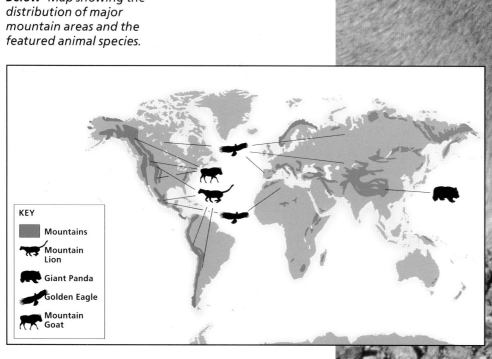

KEY

- Mountains
- Mountain Lion
- Giant Panda
- Golden Eagle
- Mountain Goat

MOUNTAIN LION

*These magnificent cats – known as
pumas, cougars, or mountain lions – are
resourceful and adaptable, and survive
even after years of persecution.*

The biggest cat in North America, the mountain lion is also one of the most widespread of all the world's cats. It can live in high mountains, conifer woodlands, tropical forests, grassland, and dry scrub from southern Canada down almost to the southern tip of South America. Within this huge area its coat may vary from light brown or tawny to gray-brown or even black, and its weight from less than 100 pounds to more than 200 pounds.

As they stumble from their den for the first time, the new cubs have light fur with brownish black spots on the body and dark rings on the tail. Their spots-and-rings fur pattern keeps them well camouflaged among the shadows. The cubs' head is small and round, and their body long and slender. The only clues to the cubs' future life as large predators are their sharp teeth and long claws.

Mountain lions are born in summer in the temperate parts of their range, and at any time in tropical areas. Their home is a den among the rocks or under tree roots, or deep in thick vegetation. The mother has used the den regularly to rest and sleep, so she knows it is relatively safe. Cubs are born with eyes and ear canals closed. They actually first experience the world at 10 to 14 days. The mother feeds her babies on milk, and she defends them against any predators, including other mountain lions, hawks, and big snakes.

Home range

Each mountain lion has its own territory, anywhere between 30 and 100 square miles. It may overlap with the territories of other mountain lions, but these cats seem to avoid each other by using overlapping parts of the territory at different times. So apart from the family, the babies rarely see others of their kind.

By the age of six or seven weeks, the cubs begin to test their teeth on solid food, which their mother catches for them. She hunts at dusk and dawn, taking deer, hares and rabbits, rodents such as rats, birds, and the occasional farm animal.

As the cubs grow, they lose their spots and rings, and develop the adult color. They practice pouncing and leaping on each other. Soon they follow their mother on twilight hunting forays. The mountain lion is a powerful yet agile creature. It can jump a 20-foot gap, spring 15 feet upward, and leap 50 feet to the ground, as well as climb trees.

Between one and two years of age, the young mountain lions leave their home range and try to establish their own territories.

Above *Cubs know by instinct that they must stay relaxed and silent as their mother moves them after a disturbance.*

Opposite *A kittenish look from a young cub.*

BABY FACTFILE

ANIMAL
Mountain lion, cougar, puma, panther

SCIENTIFIC NAME
Felis concolor

DISTRIBUTION
The Americas

SIZE OF MOTHER
Regional variations; length of head and body 3-4 feet, tail 2-3 feet; weight usually 100-180 pounds

LENGTH OF PREGNANCY
13-14 weeks

NUMBER OF BABIES
2-4

SIZE AT BIRTH
Length of body about 8-12 inches

EARLY DEVELOPMENT
Baby fur has spots and dark rings; eyes open at 10-14 days; cubs suckle for 6-7 weeks

WHEN INDEPENDENT
1-2 years

WHEN ABLE TO BREED
2-3 years

GIANT PANDA

The giant panda is instantly recognizable as a symbol of wildlife conservation. Yet knowledge of its life in the wild is still scanty.

Giant pandas are extremely rare. Probably less than 1,000 survive in the wild. They live in cool, dense bamboo forests in the hills and mountains of a very restricted area in China. Pandas are slow and deliberate in their movements. They dwell largely on the ground, though they are good tree climbers. They lead quiet lives, munching bamboo leaves and stems. They may occasionally try grasses and flowers, and small creatures such as insects.

Being rare, quiet, and elusive, giant pandas are difficult to study in the wild, and much of our knowledge about their lifestyle and breeding habits

Below *Pandas in the wild are notoriously difficult to photograph. This mother nurses her tiny month-old cub at Hetauping breeding center, Wolong Reserve.*

Above *A young panda at the famous Wolong Station, Wolong Reserve, Sichuan, China.*

BABY FACTFILE

ANIMAL
Giant panda, panda bear, bamboo bear

SCIENTIFIC NAME
Ailuropoda melanoleuca

DISTRIBUTION
Mountains of central and western China

SIZE OF MOTHER
Length of head and body 4-5 feet, tail 5 inches; weight 200-250 pounds

LENGTH OF PREGNANCY
19-20 weeks

NUMBER OF BABIES
Usually 1 cub

SIZE AT BIRTH
Length 4-6 inches; weight 3-5 ounces

EARLY DEVELOPMENT
Born helpless with eyes closed; eyes open at 6-8 weeks; weaned at 6 months

WHEN INDEPENDENT
About 1 year

WHEN ABLE TO BREED
Females at 4-5 years, males at 6-7 years

has come from observations in zoos. But the pandas' behavior in the wild may be different from that in captivity.

Male and female pandas live alone, apart from a brief courting and mating in April to May. They communicate by scent and whinelike calls. After mating, the pair split up again. The mother panda gives birth to her baby about 19 to 20 weeks later, in a den.

It is thought that a mother panda can rear only one cub. Occasionally she gives birth to two or, rarely, three, but the extra ones are ignored and soon die. The newborn is very small, weighing only 5 ounces – about as much as a large apple. It is also helpless and its eyelids are closed. The mother cleans it, keeps it warm, and feeds it on her milk. The cub's eyes open by two months of age, and it is moving around after three months.

About six months after birth, the young panda starts switching from milk to adult foods. Pandas are unusual animals in that they have a "sixth finger." This is a wrist bone that has become longer. It can be pressed against the fingers, in the way we use our thumbs. The panda uses it to grip slender leaves and shoots of bamboo.

Above *Most panda breeding information has come from captive animals, such as this youngster in Chengdu Zoo, Sichuan, China.*

By one year of age, the young panda is ready to leave its mother. It must establish its own area of territory in the hilly bamboo forests. This is difficult: Some of the regions where pandas live are being taken over by people, for villages and farmland – even though the panda is protected by world wildlife laws.

Rising star

The panda was hardly known until the 1930s, except to the people who lived near its mountainous bamboo-forest home in the Chinese provinces of Szechuan, Shensi, and Kansu. Then a few pandas were sent from China to zoos in the United States and other countries. Since they were so rare, attempts were made to breed them in captivity. The attempts attracted increasing public interest.

The giant panda has become ever more famous. It is the symbol of the Worldwide Fund for Nature's campaign to conserve animals, plants, and natural places. Yet it remains one of the rarest and most mysterious large mammals on Earth.

GOLDEN EAGLE

When the golden eagle chick emerges from its egg, it has tiny wings, a head almost too heavy to hold up, and bedraggled-looking baby feathers.

A newly hatched golden eagle does not look much like the adult it will become – the powerful, majestic "King of the Mountains." The chick is covered in straggly down, its head and beak seem too large for the scrawny body, and its wings are mere hand-sized fleshy flaps by its sides.

Six months later, the transformation is astonishing. The young eagle has a powerfully hooked beak and fearsome razor-sharp talons, or claws. It can soar for long periods on its immense wings.

Golden eagles dwell in large areas of high bushland, scrub, moor, and mountain forest. They can also survive in grassland, scattered woodland, and along shorelines.

A male and female pair for life. They occupy a large territory, perhaps over 15 square miles, where they hunt by day. Their main prey are rabbits, hares, and birds such as grouse and ptarmigan. Golden eagles also feed on carrion, from dead deer to sick and dying lambs. Sometimes an eagle is spotted feeding on a farm animal, but the eagle may not have killed it. The animal may have died from other causes, providing the eagle with an opportunistic meal.

Golden eagles also hunt other animals, especially when their normal prey is scarce. These include fish, frogs, foxes and stoats, snakes, mice and voles, and even tortoises. Their varied diet is one reason why golden eagles have easily adapted to a wide range of habitats providing a diversity of prey. Because of this fact, golden eagles are among the largest birds of prey.

Preparing the aerie

In spring, the male and female perform spectacular courtship flights near the nest site. Their courtship rituals display swooping, diving, and rolling aerials.

The nest is called an aerie and has probably been used for years. It is a huge pile of twigs and sticks, along with ferns, heather, and whatever else is available. Most aeries are high on a mountain or cliff ledge, or at the top of a tall tree. Some pairs have several nests that they reuse over the years.

The eagles repair the aerie and install a lining of grasses and rushes. The female lays two large eggs, which are white flecked with red, brown, and gray. She sits on them to keep them warm during incubation. Her mate brings the occasional meal and he may sit on the eggs for a short time.

When the baby eaglets hatch, they are already covered with down and their eyes are wide open. But they are virtually helpless. The parents – chiefly the

Above *A parent flies in to feed the offspring in their stick-twig nest, or aerie, perched perilously on a rocky ledge.*

BABY FACTFILE

ANIMAL
Golden eagle

SCIENTIFIC NAME
Aquila chrysaetos

DISTRIBUTION
Across most lands of the northern hemisphere, south to north Africa, and Mexico, mainly in upland scrub, mountain, and forest

SIZE OF MOTHER
Length 30-36 inches from head to tail; wingspan more than 7 feet

LENGTH OF INCUBATION
6-6½ weeks

NUMBER OF BABIES
2 eggs

SIZE AT BIRTH
Length 12 inches

EARLY DEVELOPMENT
On hatching, young is down-covered with eyes open; parents feed it with torn-up meat for about 3 months

WHEN INDEPENDENT
Ready to fly and leave nest at 10-12 weeks; moves away a few weeks later

WHEN ABLE TO BREED
2-3 years

mother – feed them by tearing prey into small pieces and pushing it into their mouths.

In some golden eagle nests, there is a curious and cruel event. The older chick, which hatched first and is usually the bigger, kills its younger brother or sister. Hatching two chicks may be a form of "insurance" for the parents in case one baby sickens and dies, or is stolen by a predator.

Sole survivor

After two or three weeks, the surviving chick begins to gulp down its own food. It strengthens its beak by playing with the twigs of its nest. Later, the down feathers fall out and larger, stiffer flight feathers grow. The mother leaves the dead prey next to the aerie and the eaglet tears off swallow-sized lumps by itself. Like the adults, the eaglet makes yelping and

Above Six-week-old chicks, far from golden in their downy white feathers, spar and fence with their hooked bills.

barking noises when it is alarmed.

Around 70 to 80 days after hatching, the young eagle has all of its flight feathers. It may practice flapping its wings, standing on the edge of the nest, for several days. Finally it launches itself and takes its first soaring lesson.

Over the next few weeks, the young eagle learns to fly low over the ground, searching for food with its exceptionally sharp eyes. The white patches under its wings and tail distinguish it from the adult birds. By the fall, it will have to move away and find a territory of its own.

MOUNTAIN GOAT

Even a very young mountain goat can perform astonishing feats of agility as it skips and leaps among crags and ledges.

The white-furred mountain goats pick their way among the precipitous cliffs, glaciers, and snow-capped peaks of the Rocky Mountains and other steep slopes in North America. Within hours of birth, baby mountain goats are on the move with their mother. It is midsummer and, for a time, their high mountain home may not be very cold and gale-swept. But by the fall, these young goats will face some of the harshest conditions found in any habitat. There are biting winds, driving cold rain, sleet and deeply drifted snow, and frost and ice.

Mountain goats gain two main advantages from living in such harsh surroundings. One is the lack of predators. Only a few large carnivores, such as mountain lions, dare to venture so high up the slopes. The second advantage is lack of competition for habitat. The plant growth on the upper cliffs and screes is thin, with just a few grasses, mosses, sedges, and stunted bushes. Few large herbivores can climb so high, so the mountain goats have what little food there is almost to themselves.

Mountain goats are not true goats but belong to a group of hoofed animals called goat-antelopes. One of their closest relations is the slightly smaller chamois of Europe.

Born in a rocky shelter

The mountain goat's breeding season begins in the fall when the males challenge each other for the attention of females. Mountain goats' battles on rocky slopes are explosive and physical in contrast to deers' ritualistic courtship displays. Male mountain goats rarely come to blows, but when they do, the battle is short, serious, and sometimes bloody. They stab with their horns, and the loser may suffer severe injuries. The winner gains the right to mate with the females in the territory.

About seven months later, as the weather turns warmer for spring, the mother goat finds a sheltered place to give birth. Since there is little protection

Above *A kid perches securely on a boulder at the snow line.*

Right *A nanny (female) goat keeps watch as her kid (young) feeds.*

BABY FACTFILE

ANIMAL
Mountain goat

SCIENTIFIC NAME
Oreamnos americanus

DISTRIBUTION
Rockies and other mountains of North America, high on steep slopes, snow, and glaciers

SIZE OF MOTHER
Height 3 feet at shoulder; length 4-5 feet; weight 150-250 pounds

LENGTH OF PREGNANCY
26-28 weeks

NUMBER OF BABIES
1 or 2 kids

SIZE AT BIRTH
Height about 1 foot at shoulder

EARLY DEVELOPMENT
Kids are born fully furred with eyes open and can jump about on the rocks within an hour of birth

WHEN INDEPENDENT
4-6 months

WHEN ABLE TO BREED
1-3 years

Above Mother and youngster take a rest in a patch of winter sun.

Opposite This kid is enjoying the sunny summer warmth and vegetation near Aspen, Colorado.

from the elements at these heights, her one or two kids are usually born among the rocks. Each baby goat already has a thick, warm coat of white fur. Within an hour it is skipping among the boulders and trying its skill at leaping from crag to ledge.

Mountain goats are slow, sure-footed rock climbers. For the size of their bodies, they have thick, powerful legs and very wide hooves. The well-muscled legs can wade through deep snow. Each hoof has a hard, sharp, outer rim and a softer, spongier pad in the center, like the middle of a cat's paw. With these dual-action grippers, the goats can clamber over slippery wet boulders, loose jumbles of pebbles, and glasslike frost, snow, and ice.

The baby goat is nurtured on thick mother's milk. This provides all its food needs for the first few weeks. It jumps and scrambles through the rocks and, of course, occasionally falls. But the baby is well cushioned and insulated by its luxurious, thick, whitish, fluffy fur for survival in its harsh habitat.

As the young goat matures in summer, its baby fur is gradually replaced by the adult's double coat. This consists of the long, thick, warm "underwool" of the inner coat, protected by the thicker, yellow-tinged "guard hairs" of the outer coat. The very thick fur retains the animal's body heat, protects it from the biting winds, icy rain, and snow, and also provides excellent camouflage.

Over the following weeks, the baby begins to nibble at plant food and gradually takes less of its mother's milk. It also begins to grow its horns, which are not noticeable at birth. Both male and female goats have short, sharp, black horns about 6 to 9 inches long, but those of the male are slightly thicker.

Coming round the mountain

Through the summer, the goat family of mother and young feeds on the high summer pasture. By fall, they may be moving down the mountains as snow and ice spread down from the higher slopes. They may even descend to the bushes and trees to eat leaves and sprouting buds. Like its parent, the young goat will forage for available plants but these may lack certain minerals needed for good health. Instinctively it searches for salt licks – soft rocks or dried-out pools of water that are rich in the minerals it requires.

The young goat has to endure the deep snow and ice of midwinter as well as the usual rockfalls. It must leap clear of hungry cougars and dodge swooping eagles. If it can survive, then next year it will be back on the topmost peaks again.

GRASSLANDS AND PRAIRIES

Endless seas of waving stalks and seed heads, with only the occasional tree or bush, mean that there are few places to hide on the open grasslands. So many of the animals that make their living there are large and powerful, and well able to defend themselves, such as the elephants and rhinoceroses. Or they have extra-keen senses and are endowed with speed, like the zebra and the stilt-necked giraffe. Within minutes of birth, the babies of many grassland creatures are ready to sniff the air, spy danger on the horizon, and flee as fast as their new legs will carry them.

Right A young molting bison rests in the sun.

Below Home on the range – bison graze in Custer State Park, South Dakota.

Below Map showing the distribution of grasslands and prairies and the featured animal species.

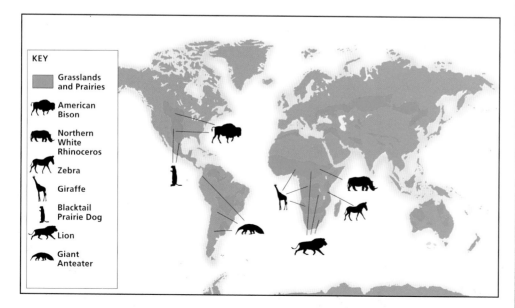

KEY

- Grasslands and Prairies
- American Bison
- Northern White Rhinoceros
- Zebra
- Giraffe
- Blacktail Prairie Dog
- Lion
- Giant Anteater

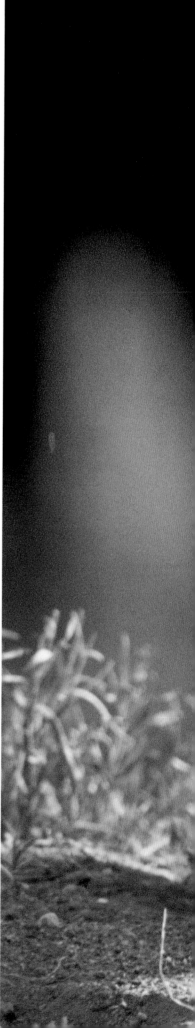

AMERICAN BISON

The fate of the bison was to become the fortune of many men. This animal's history has been inextricably linked with the settlement of North America.

When a mother bison is about to give birth, she usually leaves her group or herd, and finds a quiet place a short distance away. The calf arrives very quickly, with the mother lying on her side. It looks skinny, bedraggled, and wet because it is covered in the fluid and "bag" of membranes that protect it in the womb.

The mother tenderly licks her baby to dry it off. Licking also stimulates activity in the newborn calf, for within a few minutes the new bison can stand. Its fur dries to a fluffier, lighter, yellowish red-brown version of the adult's dark, brownish black coat. Compared to the adult, with its massive, lowering head and huge body, the baby's body is slim and its legs are long and gangly. Although slightly unsteady upon its new legs, the hungry baby begins to suckle milk from its mother. An hour or two after birth, the mother and calf rejoin the relative safety of their herd. Several days after its birth, the calf is strong enough to race and frolic with other calves, strengthening its muscles.

The young bison, or calf, stays very close to its mother for the first weeks. She will continue to suckle the calf for up to a year. After a few months, the calf begins to graze on prairie grasses. The mother bison protects her baby, even chasing away other females who are curious about the newcomer.

The calf gradually develops the longer, shaggy fur of the adult over its neck, shoulders, and front legs. Its horns begin to grow. It learns that a loud snort from a herd member signals danger, and it is ready to run like the wind at the slightest warning. Male and

Below *Mother and young, whose small, rounded horns have just begun to show.*

BABY FACTFILE

ANIMAL
American bison

SCIENTIFIC NAME
Bison bison

DISTRIBUTION
Prairies, bush, and open woodlands of North America on national parks, reservations, and private ranches

SIZE OF MOTHER
Length of head and body 8-10 feet; weight 800-2,000 pounds

LENGTH OF PREGNANCY
38-43 weeks

NUMBER OF BABIES
1 calf

SIZE AT BIRTH
Height 2-3 feet

EARLY DEVELOPMENT
Well developed at birth; can walk within minutes and move with herd after a few hours

WHEN INDEPENDENT
2-3 years

WHEN ABLE TO BREED
3 years or more; males must grow big enough to win battles with other males

Left A bison baby takes a feed from its mother.

female "subadult" young remain within the herd for two or three years.

A typical bison herd consists of a group of females, or cows, with newborn calves and yearlings. Adult males roam on the edges of the group. Young females stay in their family herd, breeding with the dominant bull. By the age of three years, most young males have left to try to establish their own dominance.

Adult males, called bulls, usually form bachelor herds. They roar and bellow loudly at each other during the summer breeding season, or rut. Bulls competing for the attention of females may have tremendous battles, crashing their heads together and trying to gouge their horns into the opponent's side. These battles establish which bulls are strongest. The most dominant can move among the females and mate with them.

Two types of bison

Many scientists think that there are two types, or subspecies, of bison: the plains bison and the wood bison. Wood bison are generally larger, with darker coats. They occupy the conifer forests of the Canadian North.

On ranches and parklands bison will rove and graze in search of fresh grasslands. As they do so, smaller groups may come together into larger herds. Bigger herds may also form at breeding time.

The history of the bison

There are few creatures more important in the history of North America than the bison. The bison played a tremendous role in the religious life of the Native American plains cultures. In addition, it provided almost all of life's essentials from meat to clothing, medicine, and tools. As a result, Native Americans always hunted in balance with nature.

When European settlers arrived in North America, it is estimated that as many as 60 to perhaps 90 million bison roamed the vast prairies and open woodlands, from the eastern Allegheny Mountains to the eastern slopes of the Rocky Mountains.

After the Civil War, there followed one of the greatest mass slaughters recorded in natural history. The bison stood no chance against the guns and greed of the newcomers eager to settle in the western United States.

However, one of the saddest and darkest periods in American history was the calculated extermination of the bison as a means of forcing Native Americans onto reservations. Both the bison and Native Americans were seen as obstacles in the settlement and development of the West. Without the bison, Native Americans would find it difficult to survive. Then the new settlers could take over the land for farms, ranches, and industries.

By the 1890s, there were only some 1,000 bison left. At last, people came to their senses, and the bison was protected by law. Parks, reserves, and refuges were set up, where today bison peacefully breed. There are more than 120,000 bison in captive breeding programs on reservations and ranches.

NORTHERN WHITE RHINOCEROS

*The birth of a baby rhino is good news,
for few animals are rarer in the wild.
However, its survival depends on its
mother's ability to evade poachers.*

The newborn of the world's second largest land animal, the white rhinoceros, is no tiny tot. The baby is small compared to its mother, who weighs almost 2 tons, but still tips the scales at up to 150 pounds.

There is something endearing about the little white rhino baby, with its too-big face and smooth nose, as it scampers to hide under its mother's enormous, lowering head. Mother white rhinos are extremely protective of their babies and will stand over them if threatened by predators. In fact, family groups will stand in a defensive formation, heads facing outward, hindquarters pressed together.

Poaching

The white or square-lipped rhino is the largest of the five rhino species. By the 1920s, it was endangered with only a few groups left throughout Africa. Since then, conservation programs such as Operation Rhino and game reserves have helped this huge, slow-growing beast to come back from the brink of extinction. However, there is no room for complacency. Poachers continue to kill the rhinos for their highly valued horns, made of compressed hairs (keratin). These are ground into "medicine" or carved into dagger handles. Many baby rhinos starve to death after their mothers have been shot.

The female white rhino mates with any male that wanders into her territory. No special bond develops between the parents. After mating, the male ambles away and takes no further part in family life.

Sometimes a few female white rhinos and their youngsters form a small group. However, the expectant mother wants to be on her own. After a pregnancy of 16 months, she looks for a quiet, secluded place. There she gives birth in the remarkably quick time of 15 minutes. The baby can stand within an hour, but it is unsteady for the first day. Within three days, it can run to and fro, and leap and play, though in a rather heavy kind of way.

The weaning period for a rhino, during which the youngster goes from drinking milk to grazing on short grasses, is one of the longest of any mammal. The baby may nibble at grass when only one or two weeks old, yet may still be nursing one year later!

At birth, the rhino has just a small, smooth bump in the place where its main front horn will grow. The horn begins to emerge at about five weeks old. By five months, it is still less than 2 inches long. Its growth is a slow process, and the final length of 2 to 3 feet is not reached for several years.

Above *The baby rhinoceros is an exact smaller copy of its parent, except for the shorter, blunter nose horn.*

Opposite *Even at a tender young age, the rhino calf's skin is thick and armorlike. Mother's bulk looms in the background.*

BABY FACTFILE

ANIMAL
Northern white rhinoceros

SCIENTIFIC NAME
Ceratotherium simum

DISTRIBUTION
Restricted parts of northeastern Africa

SIZE OF MOTHER
Height 5-6 feet at shoulder; length 10-12 feet; weight 3,000-4,000 pounds

LENGTH OF PREGNANCY
16 months

NUMBER OF BABIES
1 calf, very rarely twins

SIZE AT BIRTH
Height 18-24 inches at shoulder; weight 120-150 pounds

EARLY DEVELOPMENT
Newborn looks like miniature parent but without horn; runs with mother 3 days after birth

WHEN INDEPENDENT
Leaves mother at 2-4 years when her next calf is due

WHEN ABLE TO BREED
Females at 5 years; males at 8 years, but not usually allowed to do so by older males until at least 10 years

ZEBRA

From its first seconds, a baby zebra is at risk from big cats such as lions and leopards, dogs such as African wild dogs, and hyaenas.

The grassy plains of Africa would look much drabber without the herds of zebra mingling with the wildebeest, giraffes, and other large mammals. These striped relatives of the horse have sharp senses and fleet feet. They need these attributes because they are preyed on by a wide range of animals, from lions and leopards to hunting dogs, hyaenas, jackals, and crocodiles.

A speedy birth

Due to the many predators, a zebra's birth must be very rapid. The pregnant female leaves her group and wanders to a quiet place. She lies down and the baby, or foal, slips out easily. Within a few minutes the foal is struggling and kicking to rid itself of the "bag" of birth membranes that protected it in the womb.

In another few minutes, the foal is standing on its spindly legs. It looks like a miniature adult, with a full striped coat already grown, although the stripes are usually brown rather than almost black. The female, or mare, lies and rests for a brief period. But soon she stands up, licks the foal clean, and lets it take its first meal of milk.

The foal stays close by its mother as the two rejoin their herd. She licks and grooms the baby, having already learned to recognize it by scent. It takes the baby three or four days to learn to identify its mother in the same way. During this time, the mother drives all other animals away from the foal.

Below *Oxpecker birds will be regular companions for this zebra foal. The birds peck and snap up pests from the zebra's fur, and they will give an alarm call to alert the zebra if they spot danger.*

BABY FACTFILE

ANIMAL
Zebra, plains zebra, Burchell's zebra

SCIENTIFIC NAME
Equus burchelli

DISTRIBUTION
Grasslands of eastern Africa

SIZE OF MOTHER
Length of head and body 6-8 feet, tail 20 inches; weight 400-500 pounds

LENGTH OF PREGNANCY
52-53 weeks

NUMBER OF BABIES
1, rarely twins

SIZE AT BIRTH
Height 30-36 inches; weight 65-75 pounds

EARLY DEVELOPMENT
Newborn can stand within minutes and run after an hour

WHEN INDEPENDENT
1 year

WHEN ABLE TO BREED
Females at 2-3 years, males at 6-8 years mainly for social reasons

Above *At first the young zebra stays close to its mother, who will protect it fiercely.*

The young zebra continues to feed on milk for about six months. A week after birth, it also begins to graze on grasses and other vegetation. As the foal grows, it browses on bushes and shrubs, and eats bark. Zebras tend to feed in the morning and evening, and rest during the heat of midday and at night.

Soon the young zebra begins to take part in the social life of the herd. Zebras usually live in small groups of about five or six mares with their young and a male, or stallion. These small groups come together into loose herds, partly because there is safety in numbers.

The stallion guards his small group against predators by rearing and kicking with his powerful legs and sharp hooves. The mother protects her baby in the same way. The stallion also guards his group of mares against the attentions of other zebra males. However, as he grows older, he also becomes weaker. By 16 to 18 years of age, he is generally replaced in a peaceful takeover by a stallion of 7 or 8 years of age.

The young zebra male will probably leave his small group around his first birthday. He will join a small band, called a bachelor herd, with other young males. These young males display and fight with each other for the right to take over a group of mares from an older male. They rear up, kick and bite, and sometimes cause injury.

Young females are more likely to stay with their mother's group. They can usually start breeding in their third year.

Why stripes?

Animal experts have long argued over why the zebra has stripes. The stripes could be camouflage, especially in the half-light of dawn and dusk, when many predators are active. They could be "dazzle coloration" to confuse a predator. As zebras rush about in panic, their stripes mingle into a confusion of lines. So a predator is unable to single out one animal.

The stripes could aid in recognition. Each zebra has a unique stripe pattern, like human fingerprints. The stripes may deter flies and other pests. Or they may be "optical guides" to help one zebra groom another. Grooming helps to reinforce social bonds between group members.

GIRAFFE

The world's tallest baby is well protected by the huge kicking hooves and the swinging, battering-ram head of the mother giraffe.

A newborn giraffe is taller than most adult humans. Within an hour or two of birth, the baby is up and walking on its long, stiltlike legs, though still rather wobbly. Within two or three days it can run with the herd. It must do this because many predators lie in wait on the tree-dotted plains of Africa ready to pounce on any stragglers.

The baby giraffe has one of the best defenders in the animal world – its mother. The female giraffe, or cow, lashes out with her huge legs and hooves, and may swing her head like a battering ram. She can fight off leopards, hyaenas, and African wild dogs, and can even kill a lion with a well-aimed kick. However, predators are ever present, and about half of the baby giraffes do not reach their first birthday.

Giraffe herds consist of females and their young, and one or a few males, called bulls. These herds are very loose and informal. Almost every day, members leave and join, as the herds wander and scatter over the landscape.

In the early morning and late evening, herd members stretch up to browse on the leaves, buds, flowers, and fruits high in trees or bend down to feed on lower bushes. The giraffe can see for miles from its great height. An advantage of living in herds is that there are always likely to be one or two giraffes on

Below The world's tallest baby suckles milk from its mother.

BABY FACTFILE

ANIMAL
Giraffe

SCIENTIFIC NAME
Giraffa camelopardalis

DISTRIBUTION
Africa, grassland with scattered woods and trees

SIZE OF MOTHER
Height 13-15 feet; weight 1,500-2,000 pounds

LENGTH OF PREGNANCY
64-66 weeks

NUMBER OF BABIES
1, rarely 2

SIZE AT BIRTH
Height about 6 feet; weight 100-200 pounds

EARLY DEVELOPMENT
Baby looks like adult; can walk and run within hours of birth

WHEN INDEPENDENT
15-20 months, though may stay with mother's group for 3-4 years

WHEN ABLE TO BREED
Females by 5-6 years; males by 4 years, but not usually able to defeat rival males until 7-10 years

the lookout for predators as the others feed. During the heat of midday, they stand or lie in the shade, chewing the cud like cattle and other ruminants.

Calving grounds

When a mother giraffe is ready to give birth, she leaves the herd and visits a calving ground, which she has probably used before. It may be a grassy knoll, a tree thicket, or a small, steep valley. It is not clear how giraffes choose these traditional calving grounds. Possibly the mothers have become familiar with the place and so can better detect danger there.

The baby, usually born at dawn, is a small version of its parents. Its furry coat has the typical "network" of white or pale lines on a brown background. The mother feeds her baby in the quiet calving ground for a few days.

Peculiar features of giraffes are the two pairs of skin-covered horns on the forehead. The baby giraffe has these at birth, though they lie flat on the head. They become upright and harder during the first week, and grow slowly through most of life.

When the calf is one or two weeks old, mother and baby rejoin the herd. The calves stay together in a group. Again, there is safety in numbers. A mother may leave occasionally to catch up on feeding, but there are usually other adults nearby. Despite their

tender age, the babies are very alert and fast moving. They bleat loudly as soon as they feel threatened, and the mothers come running. Older offspring and adults can lope along at 30 miles per hour for several minutes, outpacing most predators.

The period of suckling, or feeding on mother's milk, is variable in giraffes. This may be linked to the amount of food available in the area. Some calves are fed by their mothers for more than a year. A few begin to eat leaves after only several weeks. They practice curling the long, muscular tongue around soft leaves and shoots.

Bachelor bands

A young female giraffe often stays in her mother's group. Males tend to move away by three or four years of age and join all-male juvenile groups, or "bachelor herds." Newcomers establish their position in the bachelor herd by a type of neck-wrestling called necking. Two giraffes stand near each other, twine their necks together, and push and sway to and fro, as they test each other's strength. A male must usually wait until he is fully grown, at about eight years, before he is strong enough to win the necking bouts. Then he becomes a dominant male and wins the right to court and mate with females.

BLACKTAIL PRAIRIE DOG

Named for their barks, yips, and other communicating calls, prairie dogs are actually ground-living members of the squirrel group.

For the first weeks of its life, the baby prairie dog sees no daylight. Its eyelids remain closed until about 33 days after birth. Even when they open, there is little daylight to see, because the baby is 10 or 15 feet below ground. It lies with its brothers and sisters, snug in a nest of grasses and leaves, in a nursery room that is part of a tunnel system. The mother comes down to feed her babies and then returns to the surface to feed herself.

The babies, or pups, do not usually emerge from their tunnel until they are at least one month old. By this time they are beginning to take less of their mother's milk – or the milk of other females. Any adult female in the prairie dog family may suckle the youngsters. This feeding by "foster mothers" is part of the prairie dogs' complicated and fascinating social life.

Sociable squirrels

Prairie dogs are ground-living members of the squirrel group. These stocky creatures are among the most social of all mammals, living together and communicating in many ways. The basic prairie dog group is the coterie, or extended family. It contains typically one male, one to four females, and several of their young of various ages.

The coterie has its own burrows, tunnels, rooms, and chambers. If neighbors intrude, the coterie members will defend it by rearing up on back legs,

BABY FACTFILE

ANIMAL
Blacktail prairie dog

SCIENTIFIC NAME
Cynomys *spp.*

DISTRIBUTION
Grasslands, prairies of central and western North America

SIZE OF MOTHER
Length of head and body 12 inches, tail 3-4 inches; weight 1-2 pounds

LENGTH OF PREGNANCY
4 weeks

NUMBER OF BABIES
Average 3-5, rarely up to 10

SIZE AT BIRTH
Length about 1-2 inches

EARLY DEVELOPMENT
Born naked and helpless with eyes closed; eyes open by 5 weeks; weaned at 7 weeks

WHEN INDEPENDENT
3-6 months

WHEN ABLE TO BREED
12-15 months

Below A young black-tailed prairie dog peeps out before emerging from its apparently oversized burrow.

pointing their noses to the sky, and uttering a two-part yip call. However, very young pups who wander from one coterie to another are not warned away. Adult neighbors may even play with the youngsters until their parents call them back.

Prairie dogs sleep by night in their burrow. They come out for much of the day to feed on grasses, seeds, and other plant material. The members of a coterie meet to nuzzle and chatter many times daily to strengthen their family friendships. They check who they meet by touching noses and mouths in a "kiss." If it is a friend, they groom each other to get dirt and pests out of the fur. The adults play with the youngsters, rolling and tumbling. Then they spread out and resume feeding.

Wards and towns

An average coterie covers an area of about one acre. Several neighboring coteries form a larger group called a ward. And several adjacent wards make up a town. Each coterie is usually connected to the town by a tunnel system.

Nowadays, a prairie dog town may contain thousands of individuals and cover half a square mile, but in the past their numbers were much greater. In 1900, one gigantic town was measured at over 200 miles long and 100 miles wide. It contained an estimated 400 million prairie dogs. Since then, millions of these creatures have been shot, trapped, and

Above Burrow mates sniff as they stand on the craterlike rim around their home tunnel. Prairie dogs have relatively small ears for their group, an adaptation to their burrowing lifestyle.

poisoned because their habitat was converted to farmlands and cattle ranges.

As the young prairie dogs grow bigger, they help to maintain and mend the circular mound of earth, about 2 feet high, around the burrow entrance. The mound serves as a vantage point. It also keeps out flood water and acts as a low "chimney" to aid air circulation through the burrows.

Another task is to watch for predators. Prairie dogs are hunted by coyotes, wolves, wild cats, and birds of prey. However, they have an effective early warning system. When the lookout detects danger, it utters the shrill yiplike warning barks that gave these animals the "dog" part of their name. Neighbors help to warn each other, and within seconds all the prairie dogs have disappeared below ground. Usually only the slow movers, the old or sick, are caught.

Youngsters also practice communicating with the many prairie dog calls. Barks of different notes, from low to high, indicate different messages. These include possible danger, immediate danger, all clear, and stay away from my territory!

LION

The "king of beasts" begins life as a cute and cuddly cub. Only its huge paws and claws give clues to its future size and hunting prowess.

Life seems easy for the lion group, called a pride. The pride members laze and sleep in the shade of a tree on the wide-open grasslands, or savannas, of Africa. Every few days the lionesses set off together on a hunt, usually for a large animal such as a zebra or antelope.

The male lion, with his impressive shaggy mane, rarely joins the hunt. His job is to defend the pride and mark its territory, which may be over 150 square miles. He patrols the boundary, roaring at enemies, leaving scent markers, and occasionally fighting off rivals and intruders.

Above *Playful cubs nip the huge male's tuft-tipped tail.*

Right *A king in the making.*

Sociable cats

Lions are the most sociable of the big cats. A typical pride consists of several related females and their youngsters, plus a few adult males. The males may be related to each other, but usually not to the females. Within a pride, the lions live in small "friendship" groups of about three or four individuals.

This social life extends to breeding. Lion cubs may be born at any time of year. They are small and helpless at birth, with their eyes closed. Their short fur has a spotted pattern that provides good camouflage among the shadowy grass stems and bushes. They are fed milk for up to six months by their mother and also by other pride females. Three or even four females share suckling and cub-care.

While the pride rests, the cubs tumble and play. Their games look fun, but they are training for the life of a predator. The cubs pounce on each other or on the swishing tail of an adult, trying out their claws and teeth. They strengthen their muscles, sharpen coordination, and practice stalking. When the lionesses move off to hunt, the young stay behind with two or three adult "baby-sitters."

The lion is the "king of the beasts," a powerful hunter with no natural predators. Yet four out of five lion cubs die before they are two years old. This is because in the wild, animals have natural checks or

BABY FACTFILE

ANIMAL
Lion

SCIENTIFIC NAME
Panthera leo

DISTRIBUTION
Central, eastern, and southern Africa; tiny population in India

SIZE OF MOTHER
Length of head and body about 8 feet, tail 3 feet; weight 250-300 pounds

LENGTH OF PREGNANCY
14-17 weeks

NUMBER OF BABIES
1-5, usually 2-3

SIZE AT BIRTH
Length 8-12 inches; weight less than 2 pounds

EARLY DEVELOPMENT
Newborn have closed eyes and short, spotted fur; suckle mother's milk for up to 6 months but start to eat meat at 3 months

WHEN INDEPENDENT
1-2 years

WHEN ABLE TO BREED
3-4 years (2 in captivity)

Right There is rarely a moment's peace for the mother lion. This lioness carries one cub by the scruff of its neck while another hauls playfully on her tail.

constraints on their numbers. The chief one is usually the scarcity of prey.

From about three months of age, the cubs start to eat meat. If the hunt is successful, the mother returns and leads her offspring to the kill. By four or five months old, the young lions are big and strong enough to follow the hunt.

When the cubs crowd around a fresh kill, they are often pushed away by the adults – even by their own mother. They have to wait until the rest of the pride has had sufficient nourishment. When prey is plentiful, there is enough food for cubs, and they grow and thrive. When prey is scarce, though, the cubs are the first to starve and die. This makes sense, since the survival of the pride depends on the adults remaining strong enough to hunt and defend their territory.

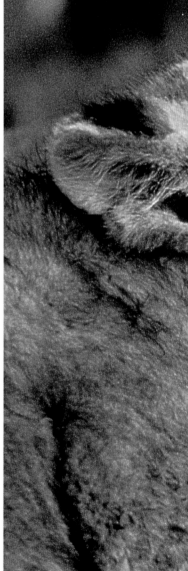

Right A cub flinches submissively as a female shows her displeasure.

Below Mother and baby settle down at last to rest in the sun.

GIANT ANTEATER

Riding piggyback on its mother across the South American grasslands, the young anteater is surely one of the most peculiar-looking animal babies.

The giant anteater is an extraordinary animal, adapted for an amazing life. It has an excessively long snout, a thin head, huge arms, and an extravagant fanlike tail. It spends its time wandering the plains, swamps, and forests of Central and South America, searching for ants' nests and eating the occupants. The giant anteater particularly likes large carpenter ants, and avoids big-jawed biting types such as army ants. It may also feed on an occasional piece of ripe fruit or a juicy grub.

This unusual-looking mammal has no teeth at all, but it possesses a very long, flexible tongue that can poke out 2 feet beyond its lips. The tongue darts out twice a second, and its coating of thick, sticky saliva, catches ants like flicking flypaper. It rubs them against the hard roof of its mouth and swallows.

The anteater breaks its way into an ants' nest using the huge claws on its fingers, wielded by the powerful, well-muscled hands and arms. Having exposed the ants, it does not feast on the entire colony. Instead, it may take only a few hundred members. The remaining ants soon repair the damage to the nest and replace their numbers. So the anteater can stop at the same nests again and again for snacks.

Adult anteaters live alone, except in the case of a mother with her young. She mates briefly with a male, and about six months later she is ready to give

Below The young anteater rides on its mother as she forages in the grassy "cerrado" vegetation of Brazil.

BABY FACTFILE

ANIMAL
Giant anteater

SCIENTIFIC NAME
Myrmecophaga tridactyla

DISTRIBUTION
Grasslands, scrub, and woods of Central and South America

SIZE OF MOTHER
Length of head and body 3-4 feet, tail 2-3 feet; weight 40-50 pounds

LENGTH OF PREGNANCY
27-28 weeks

NUMBER OF BABIES
Usually 1

SIZE AT BIRTH
Total length 16-20 inches

EARLY DEVELOPMENT
Born fully furred, looking like parent; walks and runs soon after birth; weaned at 6 months

WHEN INDEPENDENT
About 2 years

WHEN ABLE TO BREED
2-3 years

birth. She stands almost upright, propping herself up at the back with her tail. The baby appears, and almost at once it crawls up her long fur and onto her back, where it clings with its long claws. She then licks the baby clean and goes on her way.

Piggyback baby

The baby anteater looks like a small adult even from birth. Like any mammal, its first food is mother's milk. Mother and young follow a wandering life. They are active by day, with the baby riding piggyback. When it becomes old enough to walk, the baby learns the curious shuffling gait of the adult, taking the weight on its knuckles and the sides of its hands. This keeps the nest-ripping claws out of the way and sharp. If separated from its mother, the youngster will whistle shrilly for her.

Above *The extraordinary snout of the anteater is tipped by a tiny mouth, but it houses a very long, flexible, and sticky tongue.*

At night, the two sleep in a sheltered place such as a hollow or an abandoned burrow. The mother wraps herself and the baby in her great tail for protection and camouflage. If a predator, such as a jaguar, passes by, she will rear up and slash with her powerful arms and long claws.

The young anteater stops feeding on its mother's milk at about six months old, but stays with her long past that time. It may still be riding piggyback at two years of age, when it is almost as big as she is. This led to a mistaken belief that two adult anteaters took a very long time to mate! Eventually, the juvenile becomes too big and leaves.

SCRUBLANDS AND DESERTS

Some deserts are so baking hot that the rocks burn an animal's skin. Some are so freezing cold that few creatures can survive in the open. Others are both hot and cold because the sun blazes down by day, and at night the warmth floats away and temperatures plummet. But, by definition, all deserts are dry.

The dry scrub, arid bush, semi-desert, and true desert are among the toughest habitats for wildlife. With little water available, the plants are sparse and so animals are scarce. Babies of animals such as kangaroos and ostriches face great threats from the harsh conditions as well as from predators.

Below Map showing the distribution of scrublands and deserts and the featured animal species.

Right A female coyote allows her pups to play-maul her on the dry, stony ground just outside the den.

KEY

Scrublands and Deserts

Coyote

Gray Kangaroo

Cheetah

Ostrich

American Badger

COYOTE

The mournful howls of a coyote seem to suggest a lonely creature. However, these social canids are devoted to their mates and also practice cooperative behavior.

Many movies about the Wild West use the mournful howl of the coyote echoing across darkening prairies and deserts. This canine's name comes from the Aztec word *coyotl*. In the folklore of Native Americans, coyotes are often portrayed as solitary, cunning tricksters.

In the past hundred years, coyotes have expanded their range. They now live across much of North America, from Alaska and Canada down through Mexico to Central America. In contrast, their close and very similar relative in the dog family, the wolf, has become much scarcer.

In many parts of their range, coyotes live in pairs. These breeding pairs stay together for life and usually mate in late winter. The babies, called pups, are born about 63 days later. Their home is the pair's den, a large burrow up to 30 feet long and 2 feet wide. The parents keep the den extremely clean and make a dry nest from grasses, leaves, and fur.

Coyote pups develop in a similar way to wolf pups and domestic dog puppies. They are blind and help-less at birth, with short, velvety fur. The female looks

Above An older coyote pup stares suspiciously from its small den among the tree roots.

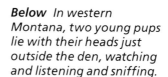

Below In western Montana, two young pups lie with their heads just outside the den, watching and listening and sniffing.

BABY FACTFILE

ANIMAL
Coyote

SCIENTIFIC NAME
Canis latrans

DISTRIBUTION
Woodland and open country across much of North and Central America

SIZE OF MOTHER
Height 18-21 inches; length of head and body 30-40 inches, tail 12-15 inches; weight 20-30 pounds

LENGTH OF PREGNANCY
9 weeks

NUMBER OF BABIES
5-8 pups, occasionally over 15

SIZE AT BIRTH
Length 3-5 inches

EARLY DEVELOPMENT
Born helpless with eyes closed; fed by mother for 5-7 weeks

WHEN INDEPENDENT
6-7 months

WHEN ABLE TO BREED
1 year

Above *This older pup has larger ears and a longer muzzle than the youngsters opposite.*

after them and feeds them on her milk, while the male goes out hunting and brings back food for her.

The pups grow steadily; their fur thickens, and their eyes open. Soon they are able to crawl around. At about three weeks of age, they begin to eat food that has been partly digested by the parents in their own stomachs. The parents regurgitate, or bring up, this food for the pups.

Family hunting trips

Once the pups are strong enough, they play outside the den, guarded by the parents. The youngsters creep and pounce on each other, gradually honing the skills that they will need for hunting when adults. Their main predators at this stage are wolves, mountain lions, and eagles.

As further practice, the whole family goes on hunting trips. The pups watch, try on their own, and learn. Coyotes hunt mainly rats and other rodents, rabbits and hares, birds, small deer, and sometimes farm stock such as lambs. The pups begin with insects, mice, and frogs. Most coyotes will also scavenge on any carcass they find.

At the age of six or seven months, the young coyotes are almost fully grown and ready to fend for themselves. They may leave their parents and travel up to 100 miles to meet a mate and set up a new family. Or they may stay with their parents and help to raise next year's pups. In this way, a coyote group, or pack, may form.

It used to be thought that these wild dogs only lived alone or in pairs. Now we know that they sometimes form packs. Coyote packs are neither as well organized nor as stable as those of wolves. But they do allow the adults to share pup-rearing duties. Any member of the pack may regurgitate food for the young. The pack may also cooperate in hunting larger prey such as deer.

Flexible, adaptable behavior is the reason for the coyote's success. Its close association with humans provides it with a varied, opportunistic diet and has increased its range to suburban and urban habitats.

GRAY KANGAROO

A large adult gray kangaroo is taller than a man. Yet the new baby is smaller than your thumb and spends weeks in the pouch before peeking out.

The gray kangaroo is one of the biggest of the kangaroos. Its powerful back legs enable the kangaroo to bound along at 25 miles per hour for long periods, sprint at over 30 miles per hour, and leap 25 feet in a single jump. Yet the newborn kangaroo is smaller than your thumb. And its legs are so poorly developed that it cannot move them at all! The new

baby has no fur, and its eyes are closed. Just about all it can do is use its stubby, paddle-shaped arms to "swim" through its mother's fur. It travels to the pouch on her belly and fixes its mouth onto a teat to suckle the mother's nourishing milk.

This extraordinary start in life happens because the kangaroo is a pouched mammal, or marsupial,

Left *A young joey among aptly named kangaroo-paw flowers.*

BABY FACTFILE

ANIMAL
Gray kangaroo, eastern gray kangaroo, forester

SCIENTIFIC NAME
Macropus giganteus

DISTRIBUTION
Open woodlands and scrub throughout eastern Australia

SIZE OF MOTHER
Height 4-5 feet; weight 100-150 pounds

LENGTH OF PREGNANCY
About 5 weeks

NUMBER OF BABIES
Usually 1, rarely twins

SIZE AT BIRTH
Length less than 1 inch; weight 1/20th ounce

EARLY DEVELOPMENT
Tiny youngster crawls to mother's pouch, attaches to teat, and stays for several months as it completes development

WHEN INDEPENDENT
12-14 months

WHEN ABLE TO BREED
2-3 years

like the koala and opossum. In other mammals, known as placentals, the babies grow mostly in the mother's womb. Some can walk and run almost as soon as they are born. In a marsupial, the baby develops for only a short time in its mother's womb. The initial period of growth and development happens after birth as the youngster remains safe and warm in its mother's pouch.

A mobile home

A young kangaroo is known as a joey. It is usually born during summer, but gray kangaroos can breed at any time of year if conditions are suitable. For the first few months, the baby does not come out of the pouch at all. Its fur slowly grows, and its eyes open. Forelimbs develop five-clawed digits and hindlimbs develop long feet with two major clawed toes. Milk provides all of its nourishment. The mother regularly cleans droppings and other debris out of her pouch.

Meanwhile the mother continues her normal life. Kangaroos live in groups called mobs, which hop through the woodlands and scrub of eastern Australia. They feed mainly at night, on grasses and leaves. By day they rest and sleep in the shade of the trees.

Safe from danger

After about six months, the baby is big enough to leave the pouch for short periods. It then looks like a small version of its parents. The joey soon hops back into the pouch if danger approaches or if the mob moves to new feeding grounds.

Life is fairly easy for the young kangaroo. These animals have few natural predators and the adults can kick fiercely to defend themselves. Gradually the joey begins to graze on grasses and other plants, and suckles less of its mother's milk. By about ten months of age, it is too large to get back into the pouch. However, for another two or three months, it can stick its head into the pouch and drink some milk.

By its first birthday, the young kangaroo is almost fully grown. It stays with its mother for several months longer, feeding, resting, and traveling with the mob. By the age of two or three, it is able to start a family of its own.

Above *A female and her offspring show the use of the pouch, or marsupium, after which the marsupial group of animals is named.*

CHEETAH

The cheetah can outsprint any prey over a short distance. Cubs must learn that if their initial dash fails, they cannot pursue prey at speed over long distances.

BABY FACTFILE

ANIMAL
Cheetah

SCIENTIFIC NAME
Acinonyx jubatus

DISTRIBUTION
Africa, Middle East, and southwest Asia

SIZE OF MOTHER
Length of head and body 4 feet, tail up to 3 feet; weight 90-130 pounds

LENGTH OF PREGNANCY
13-14 weeks

NUMBER OF BABIES
1-8, average 3

SIZE AT BIRTH
Length of head and body 8-12 inches; weight 8-16 ounces

EARLY DEVELOPMENT
Eyes open at 2-10 days; at 5-6 weeks old, cubs follow mother and begin eating meat

WHEN INDEPENDENT
About 1½ years

WHEN ABLE TO BREED
2-3 years

B aby cheetahs have long, almost silky hair, which is dark below and light gray-blue on the top of the head, neck, and back. With their rounded faces and short legs, these fluffy bundles bear little resemblance to the adult cheetah. The adult's enormously long legs and slim, supple body make the cheetah the fastest land animal in the world.

The female and male cheetah live apart, only meeting for a day or so to mate. The two yelp as they approach and court each other, and they mate several times. Then the male leaves to live alone or with a group of other males.

Right *Cheetah cubs suckle from their mother, who seems almost too thin to provide such plentiful milk.*

Opposite *The cute, rounded, kittenlike face of a baby cheetah.*

Right *A mother cheetah stalks across the newly green, rain-refreshed landscape as her trio of cubs struggle to keep pace.*

Opposite *Cubs pause in a rare piece of shade on the African scrubland.*

Cheetahs mate at almost any time of year, so the births are spread through the year, too. The new cubs have their eyes closed, and they usually open by the age of a week. The mother spends the first few days with the babies, feeding them on her milk.

After a week or two, the cubs have learned to lie quietly in a sheltered place while their mother goes out hunting. They stay hidden in the thickest vegetation she can find. The mother moves them every few days, to avoid the attention of predators. The cubs' fur color, and their habit of crouching low and still, help to make them almost invisible, even in open grassland and semidesert where undergrowth is scarce. Their main problem at this time is the relentless sun. If the youngsters stray from their patch of shade, they may die of thirst and heatstroke.

Hot pursuit

Cheetahs now occupy only a small portion of African habitat, mainly sparse woodlands and savannas. However, they prefer open country, where they can use their immense sprinting speed to full advantage. There must be enough scrub and undergrowth to conceal their slow stalk toward a victim.

Their typical prey is a small gazelle, impala, or wildebeest. At the last moment, the cheetah dashes from cover and sprints faster than any other animal, exceeding 65 miles per hour for a few seconds. The chase is short – on average, under 30 seconds and covering less than 200 yards. The cheetah overtakes its prey, biting the underside of the throat, shutting the windpipe, and causing death by strangulation.

This killing method is partly due to the cheetah's lack of long, sharp claws. Unlike most other cats, its claws are nonretractable. This means they cannot be drawn into toe sheaths to keep them protected and sharp. So the claws are shorter and blunter, unlike those of most cats, and are rarely used as hunting weapons. The cheetah's teeth are also relatively short, even the spearlike canines.

In about half of all chases, the prey manages to get away, frequently by swerving. The cheetah can swing its tail to the side to help it turn, but it is often going too fast. So it quickly gives up and conserves its energy. This big cat has tremendous speed, but little stamina.

By the age of five or six weeks, the cubs are strong enough to travel with their mother and to watch how she stalks and chases. Cheetahs have no fixed home base and roam where their prey takes them. Like all cat babies, the cubs tumble and spring at each other, developing the vital skills of the predator.

By the age of three months, the young cheetahs are no longer taking their mother's milk. They are losing their baby fur, and the adult coat, tawny yellow with small dark spots, is appearing.

The growing cubs begin to share more of their mother's kill. The main predators at this stage are vultures, hyaenas, and jackals, who may try to take over the meal. If these hungry scavengers cannot succeed in driving away the mother and her family, they may take a cheetah cub as a snack instead.

Between 15 and 24 months of age, the young cheetahs leave their mother and fend for themselves. They may stay in juvenile groups until they are ready to begin their own families, at two or three years old.

OSTRICH

Ostriches have a topsy-turvy breeding life. Several females lay eggs in the same nest, and the chicks are reared by their father.

There are many legends about the ostrich, the most famous being that it sticks its head in the sand to hide from danger! Yet the truths about the world's largest bird are stranger still. The ostrich cannot fly, but it is the fastest creature on two legs. It can run at speeds of nearly 45 miles per hour and "jog" at almost 30 miles per hour. It can also deliver devastating slashes with its two-toed, sharp-clawed feet.

Ostriches live in groups called herds, each led by a senior bird which may be male or female. The herd wanders across the African grasslands, or savannas, looking for food. The senior bird chooses the feeding grounds and decides when to move on.

Above *Newly hatched chicks gather at their nest among broken eggshells and still-unhatched siblings.*

Baby Factfile

Animal
Ostrich

Scientific name
Struthio camelus

Distribution
Dry grasslands of Africa; introduced into places such as Australia and North America to be farmed for their feathers, skin, and meat.

Size of mother
Height 6-8 feet; weight 200-240 pounds

Length of incubation
6 weeks

Number of babies
10-40 eggs per nest

Size at birth
Height 1-2 feet

Early development
Chicks hatch well developed and camouflaged; can run fast at a month old

When independent
2-3 months

When able to breed
Females at 2-3 years, males at 3-4 years

Left *A band of juvenile ostriches, not yet in adult plumage, pass by a lake in the Transvaal, South Africa.*

The breeding habits of ostriches are as curious as the rest of their lives. Ostriches can rear young at almost any time of year, generally after the rains have brought new life to the parched land.

A typical breeding group or harem loosely consists of one male and three females. Unlike many other birds, the father does most of the work. He mates with all the females. Then he prepares a nest, which is a shallow scrape about 3 feet across in the ground.

The females lay their eggs in this communal nest. Each produces 8 to 12 eggs, laid on alternate days. The dominant or senior female shades the eggs by day from the scorching African sun. The male takes over at dusk and sits on the eggs through the night.

The ostrich's egg is the biggest of any living bird. It is 6 inches long and weighs up to 3 pounds – 40 times as much as a hen's egg. The very thick shell protects against enemies, such as hyaenas and vultures.

Usually not all the eggs hatch. The father and dominant mother look after the newborn chicks, which are well developed with open eyes. Within a day or two they can walk and run, though they are

Above *These leggy youngsters are being watched over by their father. The mothers have more uniform brownish plumage.*

rather wobbly. Their soft down feathers, light fawn with darker brown spots and flecks, make them almost invisible as they crouch down and stay still among the pebbles, grasses, earth, and bushes.

The eat-anything bird

At a month old, the fluffy babies are speedy runners. All the chicks from the families in the herd may gather into a large nursery, supervised by one or two adults. The chicks peck at the ground, and they soon learn what is edible and what is not. For an ostrich, however, there is little difference. They prefer to eat seeds, stems, buds, leaves, and fruits of a wide variety of plants, but will try anything.

The young grow rapidly and molt their baby down for the "hairy" adult feathers. Soon the herd is on the move again, wandering through the savannas on the never-ending search for food and water.

AMERICAN BADGER

The squat, powerful American badger has a reputation for fighting fiercely to defend itself and its young.

There are nine kinds, or species, of badger around the world. But the only one that lives in the New World is the American badger. Like all badgers, it is a member of the weasel family, the mustelids.

In nature, the American badger has few predators. Its stocky and strong body, fearsome bite, and powerful claws all provide excellent defense. When threatened, the badger snarls, hisses, stiffens, and raises its hair to stand on end so that it looks almost twice its normal size. It may also release a strong-smelling scent from the anal glands under its tail. The badger normally smears the scent on objects in its territory to advertise its presence, marking the boundaries which it will defend furiously.

The female badger, or sow, mates with a male, or boar, in the late summer or early fall. The new babies develop inside their mother's womb for only about six weeks, yet they are born the following spring! The reason is that after being fertilized by the male's sperm, the tiny eggs begin to develop – and then stop. They stay in "suspended animation," as tiny balls of cells, for up to six months. Then the balls of cells implant, or burrow, into the lining of the womb and continue their development into baby badgers. The

---

BABY FACTFILE

ANIMAL
American badger, badger

SCIENTIFIC NAME
Taxidea taxus

DISTRIBUTION
Scrub and open, dry areas of western Canada to Mexico,

SIZE OF MOTHER
Length of head and body 16-22 inches, tail 4-6 inches; weight 10-20 pounds

LENGTH OF PREGNANCY
6 weeks, after implantation delayed 6 months

NUMBER OF BABIES
Usually 2 cubs, up to 6

SIZE AT BIRTH
Length 5 inches

EARLY DEVELOPMENT
Newborn covered with silky fur; eyes open at 6 weeks; stay underground for 6-8 weeks

WHEN INDEPENDENT
7-9 months

WHEN ABLE TO BREED
Females from 5-6 months, males from 1-2 years

Above *Like many young mammals, this badger has a rounder face and shorter snout than its parents. The "snub nose" helps when suckling at the mother's teats.*

Left *This young badger is practicing digging and nosing for food in the soft, sandy soil of the dry brushlands. Its powerful front claws are clearly shown as it pauses.*

process is called delayed implantation and occurs in several kinds of mammals, including seals and bats.

Born on a grassy bed

Badgers usually live in a burrow, sometimes known as a sett. The babies, or cubs, are born there in spring, on a soft, clean bed of grasses, leaves, and mosses. The newborn are covered with silky fur, but their eyes are not yet open.

Badgers are very clean creatures. The female regularly replaces the bedding with fresh greenery so that the babies are warm and dry. She dumps the old bedding around the burrow entrance.

The cubs' eyes open about six weeks after birth. The babies stay in the den, feeding on their mother's milk. A week or two later, the sow cautiously leads them out of the den for the first time. Badgers are active mainly at night. They may come out in daylight, but only if they are sure there is no threat. The cubs stay out for only a short time before going back underground.

After another week or so, the cubs are spending longer periods outside the den. They play and roll like puppies, watched by their mother. Gradually she takes the babies farther afield, and they learn to sniff out and catch food. The main items in their diet are mice, voles and other small rodents, rabbits, ground squirrels, and chipmunks. These animals may try to escape by burrowing, but the badger is a much faster and stronger digger. Other prey include eggs, birds, frogs, and reptiles such as lizards and snakes.

By about eight months of age, the young are ready to leave home. More and more badgers are going to live in suburbs and urban areas. They build setts in gardens and parks, and raid trash cans for food.

RIVERS AND LAKES

The surface of a lake or wide river may look quiet and serene. But beneath it there is a busy world of plants and animals that we rarely see. Fish and shellfish, which cannot survive away from water, compete for food with mammals, which can live in water or on land. These semi-aquatic mammals range from small water voles to huge hippopotamuses. In northern areas, moose chomp at the water plants, while in warmer climates, crocodiles lurk in lakes and rivers. The babies of all these animals are at risk from predators on the bank, in the air above, and in the depths below.

Right As it grows older and larger, the moose calf is able to follow its mother and wade into the lake to munch on the water plants growing just beneath the surface.

Below Map showing river and lake areas frequented by the featured animal species.

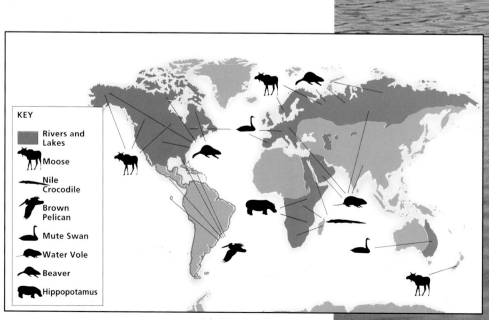

KEY

Rivers and Lakes

Moose

Nile Crocodile

Brown Pelican

Mute Swan

Water Vole

Beaver

Hippopotamus

MOOSE

The stilt-legged moose calves, with their splayed hooves and humped backs, will grow to be the largest of all the deer.

The newborn moose calf looks just like its mother, the cow, though its coat is more reddish brown. For the first two or three days the calf cannot stand or walk properly. So it lies still and silent, hidden in the undergrowth, while its mother feeds nearby. If the calf is hungry, it calls softly and the mother comes to it. She may squat or lie down so that the baby can reach her udder to drink the milk.

Moose are the largest members of the deer group. A healthy, full-grown moose is more than a match for most predators, even a small wolf pack. The huge deer kicks and tramples the enemy with its long legs and great hooves. However, the baby is at risk from wolves, mountain lions, coyotes, and perhaps bears.

Over the first few weeks the calf learns to walk and run. It follows the mother as she ranges farther in search of food. Moose are basically woodland animals and they browse on leaves from trees and shrubs, and graze on low-growing herbs and plants. After several weeks, the calf copies its mother and begins browsing for green leaves. When adult, it may need to eat 20,000 leaves each day.

Moose are experts at wading into a lake or river. There they forage for aquatic plants such as water lilies. Moose are powerful swimmers and can dive fully submerged to forage for aquatic plants.

Solitary, then social

Moose calves are born in late spring or early summer. A cow will protect her calf from all intruders. Predators, even other moose, and people on horseback have been driven off by her attack.

In the fall, moose become social animals. The bulls spar and wrestle each other with their enormous flattened antlers, and bellow loudly for females, who answer through the forest. Then the dominant bull courts and mates with the females.

After the mating season, the adult moose wander away to live apart again. The growing calves usually continue to follow the cows until they are a year or two of age. Then they, too, become solitary outside the mating season.

At about one year of age, a male calf grows "spike" antlers about 6 inches long. One or both of the antlers may fork as they gradually lengthen. Each year the antlers fall out and regrow, with more branches, or points, varying in size and shape. By the time the bull is fully grown, his pair of antlers may have 20 points and measure more than 6 feet across the tips.

Above This cow moose has produced triplets, a rare event.

Opposite With its legs still wet from its wading adventures, this calf has a bankside snack.

BABY FACTFILE

ANIMAL
Moose

SCIENTIFIC NAME
Alces alces

DISTRIBUTION
Northern North America, Northern Europe, and Northern Asia; introduced into New Zealand

SIZE OF MOTHER
Height at shoulder 5-7 feet; weight 1,000-1,200 pounds

LENGTH OF PREGNANCY
34-36 weeks

NUMBER OF BABIES
1, sometimes 2 or rarely 3 to older mothers

SIZE AT BIRTH
Height 3 feet

EARLY DEVELOPMENT
Looks like parent at birth but unable to walk for 2-3 days

WHEN INDEPENDENT
Suckles for 6 months; stays with mother for 1-2 years

WHEN ABLE TO BREED
2-3 years

NILE CROCODILE

The discovery that the mother crocodile carries and cares for her babies provides insight on this reptilian survivor from the age of the dinosaurs.

Crocodiles look like remnants from prehistoric times, when dinosaurs roamed the Earth's steamy ancient swamps, and in fact they are. Members of the crocodile group of reptiles were alive all through the age of the dinosaurs. Crocodiles and alligators are the closest living reptile relatives of those huge prehistoric monsters.

The Nile crocodile of Africa has a very relaxed lifestyle. Since it is a reptile and cold-blooded, it does not have to burn up energy to stay warm and active as birds and mammals do. It spends the night resting in the water. By day, it lurks in the water or on the bank, waiting for prey to come near. If it catches a big victim, such as a wildebeest or even a giraffe, the crocodile has enough food for several weeks.

When scientists were studying Nile crocodiles years ago, they saw that some of the adults had newly hatched babies in their mouths. Given the crocodile's reputation as a killer, they concluded that the adults ate babies of their own kind. Recent research has shown that, though cannibalism does occur, it is uncommon. Most crocodiles with new hatchlings in their mouths are mothers caring for their babies.

After mating, the female crocodile digs a pit with her rear legs in the soft bank soil near a river or lake. She lays her eggs in the pit and covers them with earth. The eggs incubate in the warm soil and the female guards them until they hatch. The male sometimes helps protect the eggs, too.

Despite this, the eggs are occasionally dug up and eaten. They may be taken by a monitor lizard, which has lured the parent away from the nest. Or they may be snatched by a mongoose, which has slipped in before the monitor lizard can return!

When the babies are ready to hatch, they respond to the footfalls of the parent above and make

Below The tiny head of a newly hatched baby crocodile pokes from between its mother's awesome, "smiling" jaws. She gently carries her babies to the water.

BABY FACTFILE

ANIMAL
Nile crocodile

SCIENTIFIC NAME
Crocodylus niloticus

DISTRIBUTION
Rivers, lakes, and swamps across much of Africa, south of the Sahara

SIZE OF MOTHER
Length 14-16 feet

LENGTH OF INCUBATION
3 months

NUMBER OF EGGS
25-75

SIZE AT HATCHING
Length 10 inches

EARLY DEVELOPMENT
New hatchlings look like tiny adults; guarded by mother for 3-6 months; grow to 3 feet long by 2 years old

WHEN INDEPENDENT
3-6 months

WHEN ABLE TO BREED
10-15 years

squeaky calls. The mother digs them out and carries them tenderly in her mouth to a "nursery pool." There she, and sometimes the male, too, look after them for up to six months.

Learning to hunt

The babies can walk and swim as soon as they hatch, and they sun themselves on the parent's back or head. They begin their hunting life with small prey, such as insects, frogs, and little fish. Later they graduate to larger fish and other big animals. They may also be eaten themselves, despite their caring parents. The variety of predators includes hunting fish, turtles, snakes, eagles, hawks, herons, mongooses, different species of cats, and sometimes older crocodiles.

Above This baby crocodile watches among water plants for the passing insect or frog that will become one of its first meals.

As they grow, the young crocodiles hide in groups, called pods, in quiet, shallow waters. At about two years of age, they move to deeper water and live in groups of about 20, avoiding the adults. By four years old, they are large enough to mingle with the adults. But they have a junior status in the group and must wait for many years before they can breed.

BROWN PELICAN

Although the brown pelican appears ungainly and unbalanced, it is a strong flier, an expert swimmer, and a spectacular high-diver.

There are eight kinds, or species, of pelicans around the world. All are large birds that live in groups by lakes, waterways, and the sea. The most noticeable feature of a pelican is its huge, balloon-like chin pouch, called the gular pouch. The bird scoops up a pouchful of water containing fish and other water creatures. It then empties out the water, but retains and swallows its fishy food.

The smallest species, and among the most familiar in North America, is the brown pelican. It winters in Florida, California, and farther south.

Above *A young chick gets its beak and pouch in a twist as it tries to swallow food, while the parent watches knowingly.*

Opposite *Older chicks on their nest in the Galápagos Islands.*

BABY FACTFILE

ANIMAL
Brown pelican

SCIENTIFIC NAME
Pelecanus occidentalis

DISTRIBUTION
Coasts of North America, Caribbean, South America, Galápagos Islands

SIZE OF MOTHER
Length from beak to tail 45-50 inches

LENGTH OF INCUBATION
4 weeks

NUMBER OF EGGS
2-3

SIZE AT BIRTH
Length of chicks 6-8 inches

EARLY DEVELOPMENT
Naked and blind on hatching; soon grow soft white down; walk at 3 weeks; fed by parents until 8-10 weeks old

WHEN INDEPENDENT
14-16 weeks

WHEN ABLE TO BREED
3-4 years

Brown pelicans rarely fill their pouch at the surface like other pelicans. Typically, they dive into the water from up to 50 feet above the surface, with their wings held back and the neck curved into an S shape. Having caught their food, they swim up to eat while floating on the surface.

Breeding in colonies

Pelicans spend most of their time in groups, and the breeding season is no exception. These heavy-bodied, huge-beaked birds nest in large colonies. There is much coming and going as they court, mate, and raise their families.

While courting, the male pelican chooses a nest site, usually in a tree or on a grassy hump of ground. He gathers nest-building material, and the female constructs the nest. Both parents take turns to sit on the eggs to incubate them, and both feed the youngsters once they have hatched.

Newly hatched baby pelicans are not very attractive to human eyes. They are helpless, with naked skin and eyes closed. Usually two or three eggs hatch, but the parents only tend one chick and the others soon die. The favored chick is kept warm, well fed, and protected. It quickly grows soft white down.

To feed its offspring, the mother or father regurgitates, or brings up, semidigested, soupy food from its own stomach. This dribbles into the chick's mouth. As the chick grows, it can thrust its own head into the parent's beak to reach the food inside.

By about three weeks of age, the chicks can waddle about. They leave their nests and gather in noisy nursery groups, known as pods. The parents continue to feed their young in the pods until they are up to ten weeks old. By this time, the youngsters have grown so rapidly that they are heavier than their parents, and they must fend for themselves. The young live on their stored reserves of body fat until they are about 12 weeks old. Then they start to fly, and soon they are catching their own food.

MUTE SWAN

*Few predators dare to intrude on the
territory of a swan pair with their
cygnets. These powerful water birds
fiercely defend their family.*

BABY FACTFILE

ANIMAL
Mute or white swan

SCIENTIFIC NAME
Cygnus olor

DISTRIBUTION
*Mainly Europe; introduced into
some other regions such as
Australia and North America*

SIZE OF MOTHER
*Length 4-5 feet from beak to tail;
wingspan up to 6 feet*

LENGTH OF INCUBATION
About 5 weeks

NUMBER OF BABIES
4-7 eggs

SIZE AT BIRTH
Length about 8-10 inches

EARLY DEVELOPMENT
*Cygnets soon leave the nest, travel
on mother's back, and learn to
swim and eat water plants*

WHEN INDEPENDENT
About 4-6 months

WHEN ABLE TO BREED
4 years

Few baby birds have such caring parents as the mute swans. These graceful, powerful birds defend their nest, and the chicks when they hatch, with fierce displays against intruders. The male, especially, hisses and folds his wings over his back, curls his neck back and down, and then rushes forward in the water, paddling with rapid surges. If this fails he may attack, pecking and beating his wings.

The "mute" swan is not really silent, since it can grunt and snort as well as hiss. It can even trumpet feebly, though more quietly than the other kinds of swans.

A pair for life

The male swan is known as a cob, and the female is called a pen. In spring, the cob takes possession of a large stretch of waterway on a sluggish river or by a pool or a lake. He defends it aggressively against other creatures. He and his mate court by waving and tossing their heads, and dipping them into the water. These courtship displays continue through the breeding season.

Mute swans pair for life. They construct a large mound-shaped nest of twigs, reeds, and sedges, and

Right *The family takes a swim in typical swan country – waterways fringed with thick vegetation.*

Opposite *Some of these chicks have hatched, while others struggle to escape from the shells.*

other water plants. The nest may be 15 feet across and 3 feet high, with a pit in the center for the eggs. It is hidden among the bankside vegetation.

The female generally lays five or six eggs, but in a good year, there may be up to a dozen. She sits on them to keep them warm while they develop, and the male keeps watch for intruders. Occasionally she goes off to feed in the shallow water or along the bank, and the cob takes a turn at incubation.

Some 34 to 38 days after being laid, the eggs hatch. The tiny chicks, called cygnets, are covered in fluffy down feathers, which are pale gray on the upper parts and white underneath. Within a day or two of the first cygnets hatching, they are dipping their feet in the water. The father watches over them as they paddle and learn to swim, while the mother sits on the remaining eggs.

Eventually the whole swan family swims around its territory, feeding and resting in the reeds. The cygnets eat soft, juicy water plants. The mother leads the group, and she pecks and uproots plants for her babies to eat. Sometimes the cygnets ride piggyback on their mother. The father is ever watchful and chases off other waterfowl, dogs, and people.

Above The female swan, or pen, incubates her eggs on the large, mounded nest.

Right The baby swan, or cygnet, sits peacefully in its nest. Its parents vigorously attack any intruders.

Becoming independent

The cygnets grow rapidly. By the age of four months, their pale gray down is replaced by a mottled mixture of brown over white feathers, suggesting a "dirtied" appearance. They have learned to dip their long necks into the water to grub for aquatic plants, such as pondweed, and worms and small shellfish from the bottom. They also eat the occasional small fish, tadpole, or water insect.

Toward the end of summer, the caring parents lose interest in their brood. Through the winter mated pairs rarely leave preferred breeding sites. The male does not bother to defend his territory outside the breeding seasons. All of the swans feed, rest, and survive in the best way they can. Next spring, the male will once more take charge of his patch of waterway, and the yearly breeding cycle will begin again.

WATER VOLE

Sometimes mistaken for a "water rat," the water vole can rear up to five litters of five babies each in a single breeding season.

This animal is sometimes misnamed the "water rat." Voles have furred tails, rounder faces, blunter noses, and smaller ears than rats. But it is difficult to tell vole from rat as the creature swims along with only its beady eyes, nose, and whiskers protruding at the surface.

Baby water voles are born into a dry, comfortable, ball-shaped nest of grasses, mosses, and leaves, in a bank burrow or hollow tree. Old birds' nests are sometimes used. Most births take place in spring and summer, although some females continue breeding until October and produce several litters of young.

Newborn voles are pink and furless, and are blind at birth. They stay in the nest and drink their mother's milk. By ten days old, their soft fur, thick and reddish gold, is appearing.

The babies grow fast; after about two weeks, their beady, black, button eyes are fully open, and they take their first cautious steps out of the nest. This is a risky time. An owl, hawk, weasel, or large rat may suddenly appear and pick up a small, squeaking bundle as its take-away meal.

The young voles paddle in the water, but they are surprisingly reluctant to learn to swim. More dangers lurk underwater in the shape of pike, eels, large trout, and even hungry otters. However, by the age of three weeks, the voles can swim and dive with ease. By then, they are weaned from their mother's milk

Below As the vole dives, water pressure squashes its fur flatter and reveals the true outline of its body. The eyes are wide open.

BABY FACTFILE

ANIMAL
Water vole

SCIENTIFIC NAME
Arvicola terrestris

DISTRIBUTION
Europe, Middle East, and western and northern Asia

SIZE OF MOTHER
Length of body 6-8 inches, tail 4-5 inches; weight 4-8 ounces

LENGTH OF PREGNANCY
3-4 weeks

NUMBER OF BABIES
Average 3-6 per litter

SIZE AT BIRTH
Length 1-2 inches; weight $\frac{1}{4}$ ounce

EARLY DEVELOPMENT
Newborn young are furless with eyes closed; eyes open by 10 days; emerge from nest at 15 days

WHEN INDEPENDENT
3-4 weeks

WHEN ABLE TO BREED
6-12 months

Left *This female vole sits with her blind, helpless new babies in an accidentally disturbed nest. Soon afterward, the family was safely relocated.*

Below *Fully furred and ready to face the world, these three older offspring follow their mother from the nest hole.*

and, like their parents, feed on plant material. This includes juicy shoots of waterweeds and other aquatic plants, grasses, reeds, nuts, and fruits.

Importance of grooming

The water vole has two coats of fur. The outer coat consists of long, coarse guard hairs, which are dark brown or nearly black. Beneath is the soft underfur of dense, short, fine hairs. The vole uses its sharp claws and teeth to remove bits of leaves, twigs, and mud from its coat. It spreads waterproofing oils through the hairs as it grooms, to keep its fur in tip-top condition.

The young water voles begin instinctively to groom their thick fur. They must learn to perfect this activity because their lives depend on it. Well-groomed fur is essential to keep in body warmth and keep out water. They enter the water to search for food, to avoid danger, or to enter their burrow network by an underwater entrance.

Should a predator appear, the whole vole group may act in defense. One young male approaches it, while the females and young move toward safety. If the enemy continues to attack, another young male enters the fight, and finally, the father may join in.

In a month or so, the youngsters leave to occupy bankside burrows of their own. If the neighborhood is already crowded, these juveniles may set off across land to search for a new home. In the fall, they are seen nosing about in damp woods and meadows. In fact, some water voles rarely see water but live in dry areas, like their smaller cousin, the field vole.

BEAVER

*Famed for their skill at tree felling,
dam making, and house building,
beavers lead a tight-knit family life.*

It is late spring in the dappled woodland of North America. Near the middle of a large, shallow pond, a mound about 7 feet across protrudes above the surface. It is made of sticks and stones, twigs and mud. This is the home, or lodge, of a family of beavers.

The beaver family has built up the lodge from the pond bed, extending and strengthening it each year. Inside is a large chamber just above the water level, with three underwater entrances. The beavers are excellent swimmers and divers, and they can come and go from the lodge without being seen.

Inside the family lodge, three new offspring, called kits, sleep on the floor of the chamber. Next to them, their mother washes her fur with her tongue and combs it with her claws to remove mud and leaves.

A cold, dark nursery

The young beavers appear warm and whiskery, with their thick fur and the long, sensitive hairs on their noses. These features are vital for survival, as the thick fur keeps the small babies warm. Inside the lodge it is dark and the beavers find their way about largely by touch, using their sensitive whiskers and agile forepaws.

Day by day the kits grow, suckling milk from their mother. She leaves them occasionally to feed outside the lodge on nutritious water plants and bark. Father

BABY FACTFILE

ANIMAL
North American beaver

SCIENTIFIC NAME
Castor canadensis

DISTRIBUTION
*Across much of North America;
introduced into parts of Europe
and Asia*

SIZE OF MOTHER
*Length of body 30-40 inches, tail
12-18 inches; weight about 40-50
pounds*

LENGTH OF PREGNANCY
15 weeks

NUMBER OF BABIES
2-4 kits, occasionally up to 10

SIZE AT BIRTH
*Length of body 12 inches, tail 3
inches; weight 1-2 pounds*

EARLY DEVELOPMENT
*Well developed at birth; feed on
mother's rich milk for about
4 weeks*

WHEN INDEPENDENT
2-3 years

WHEN ABLE TO BREED
3-4 years

Opposite *This youngster
has a mini-version of the
adult's large, flat, scaly tail.*

Below *An adult beaver
and kit in shallow water.*

Above *A kit holds onto its swimming parent's tail in this unusual view from above. The baby is about three and half weeks old.*

beaver, along with two of last year's litter, and a male youngster from the year before, also lives in the lodge. They spend their time collecting food, repairing their home, eating, and resting. They also maintain the dam, which they built across a small creek. The dammed waters have flooded out to form a wide pond, where the kits will learn to swim.

Around four weeks after birth, the parents begin to bring their youngsters small twigs and bits of bark, chiefly aspen and willow. Just inside the bark layer is spongy sapwood containing juicy, nourishing sap. The kits gnaw eagerly, exercising their strong jaw muscles and chisel-sharp incisor teeth.

A fatal encounter

A few weeks later, the kits are practicing swimming and diving in their pond. From the very beginning, they instinctively learn how to hold their breath, close their ear flaps, and kick strongly with their webbed back feet. They are also becoming skillful at gnawing the twigs and branches of trees. Gradually they learn to find the thinnest bark and the sweetest, most nourishing sapwood.

One early evening in July, the peace of the pond at dusk is broken. One of the young beavers has strayed too far. A lynx leaps from the bushes, grabs the beaver kit in her mouth, and vanishes into the woods. Immediately, the father beaver warns the rest of the family by slapping the water surface with his flat tail to make a loud "smack." Within seconds, the rest of the family is safe in the lodge.

Leaving home

By fall, the two remaining kits have grown to nearly the size of their parents. The brother born two years ago has left the family lodge to establish a new beaver group elsewhere.

Before the first frosts fall, the family busily collects woody stems to make an underwater cache near the lodge. The family members help each other to move larger branches. In deep winter, when the pond surface ices over, the beavers dive from their lodge's underwater burrows and swim to deeper water, which is not frozen. The cold water temperature preserves the woody stems' nutritional value. The two kits eat most of the winter food, while the parents live mainly on their stores of body fat.

Left A parent and two kits are inside a lodge specially adapted for photography. Branches, stones, and mud form its strong walls.

Below Mother and youngster swim out in the lake they have created for themselves by damming a stream.

HIPPOPOTAMUS

The name hippopotamus means "river horse." Hours after birth, a baby hippo can wade, swim, dive, and walk submerged along the river bed.

Hippopotamus is Greek for "river horse", and if you ever glimpse a hippo walking along a river bed, completely submerged, you will see that the name is very suitable. Huge and lumbering on land, the hippo is almost graceful underwater, seeming to bounce along virtually at a canter. Early Greek naturalists incorrectly thought the hippo was related to the horse. Today, naturalists classify the hippo as a distant relative of the pig.

The baby hippo may be born on land or in the water. The pregnant mother leaves her group, or herd, and finds a secluded place in shallow water or in bankside vegetation. If the baby is born below the surface, it paddles up to take its first gasps of air.

Some people think that hippos are ugly, with their piggy eyes, overblown cheeks, and enormously wide

Above *A new hippo calf, only one week old, snuggles up to its mother as she wades in the shallows. The calf can swim and dive almost from birth.*

BABY FACTFILE

ANIMAL
Hippopotamus

SCIENTIFIC NAME
Hippopotamus amphibius

DISTRIBUTION
Rivers and lakes near grasslands in Africa

SIZE OF MOTHER
Length of head and body 10-11 feet; weight 2,600-3,000 pounds

LENGTH OF PREGNANCY
33-34 weeks

NUMBER OF BABIES
1 calf, very rarely twins

SIZE AT BIRTH
Height 2-3 feet; weight 90-100 pounds

EARLY DEVELOPMENT
Well developed at birth; can swim and dive with mother a few hours later

WHEN INDEPENDENT
12-18 months

WHEN ABLE TO BREED
Female 7-14 years, male 5-10 years

Left *A family group of hippos of various ages basking on a sandbank in the bend of an African river.*

snouts. Other people find them rather appealing. The baby hippo, even rounder and tubbier than its parent, looks almost like an inflatable toy. Within its first hour, it begins to suckle milk from its mother. It can also run along the bank, splash through the shallows, and paddle into deeper water.

Fierce protector

Mother and baby stay by themselves for a week or two, then rejoin the herd nearby. She is very protective of her baby. If an enemy approaches, she will rush forward and open her mouth wide to reveal her lower canine teeth, which look like sharp, foot-long daggers. In addition, she can easily bowl over and trample most predators. A well-fed, full-grown hippo is the third largest land animal in the world, after the elephant and the white rhinoceros. Some females weigh over 2 tons, while big old males tip the scales at nearly 4 tons.

By day, the hippo herd lazes in the water or wallows in muddy swamps. At night, herd members

Above *Great folds of flabby skin already adorn this young calf, resting as wide-eyed as a hippo can be, next to its dozing mother.*

leave the water and split up. Individuals or mother-baby pairs move into the surrounding grasslands and feed for five or six hours.

The new baby nurses on land as well as underwater. When feeding underwater, it must swim up every few mouthfuls to breathe. The young hippo stays with its mother for about 12 to 18 months. By then it is grazing on grass during the nighttime and is weaned from its mother's milk.

If the youngster is female, it may stay with the herd, which consists mainly of female hippos and their offspring. If it is male, it will probably leave to join a group of other young males. As they mature, the males battle with each other for the territorial rights to a stretch of water and bank. Only by "owning" a patch of river or lake can a male win the right to mate with females and become a father.

SEASHORES AND SEAS

Seas and oceans cover more than two-thirds of our planet's surface. They appear fairly uniform from above, but beneath the waves, the seascape is as varied as the landscape on the continents. There are underwater mountains, sandy plains, and deep, mysterious canyons. In some areas, forests of seaweed tower up to the surface, and in others, vast coral reefs harbor a myriad of creatures. Around the edges of the oceans are beaches, dunes, mud flats, cliffs, and estuaries. Each of these habitats presents special living conditions and special problems for bringing up babies. Some sea animals, like the sea lions, turtles, and albatrosses, return to land to breed. Others, like dolphins and whales, give birth and raise their offspring entirely at sea.

Above *A young California sea lion basks on the back of a northern elephant seal.*

Below *Map showing the distribution of featured animal species around the seas and seashores of the world.*

Right *A female sea lion coaxes her pup toward the water.*

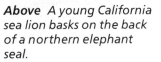

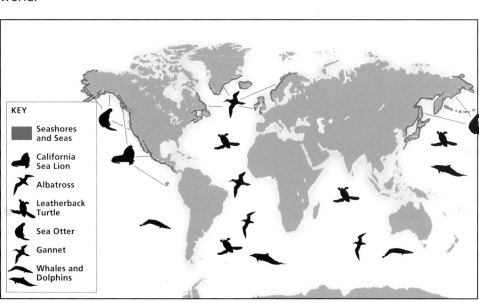

KEY

- ▬ Seashores and Seas
- California Sea Lion
- Albatross
- Leatherback Turtle
- Sea Otter
- Gannet
- Whales and Dolphins

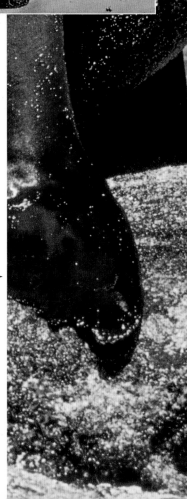

Left *Fresh from a swim, this young sea lion negotiates its way along the rocky shore.*

chestnut brown in color, although when it is wet, it looks glossy black from a distance.

Fish suppers

The young sea lions also learn other survival techniques. The most vital is fishing skills. California sea lions eat a range of items, from fish, such as salmon, to squid and octopus. They feed by day and at night, feeling in the water and along the seabed with their whiskery noses.

Most seals are not very expert at controlling their body temperature. Sometimes the young get too hot in the sun. They learn to cool off with a quick dip.

The summer passes slowly. By fall, the males have forgotten their battles over territory. They live fairly peacefully with the females and young, forming a large group known as a herd. The herd members keep a look-out for predators, primarily sharks and killer whales.

In December and January, northern seals begin to wean their pups. When next spring comes, they will be fully independent, finding their own food and trying to survive storms and predators.

ALBATROSS

The albatross has the longest wingspan of all birds and also one of the longest breeding cycles.

The baby albatross hatches onto one of the most remote places on Earth. Most kinds of albatrosses like to nest on distant rocky islands that support few animals and are rarely visited except by other birds. Albatrosses spend nearly all of their life at sea.

The new chick's tiny, stubby wings give little clue to the size they will become. Albatrosses have immense wingspans – the wandering albatross has the longest wings of any bird, up to 11 feet in some cases. The wings are very slim, and the muscles that move them are not particularly powerful. So the young albatross has great difficulty learning to take off from its island home. To help it, the parents usually build the nest on a cliff top where winds swirl and rise upward. The young inexperienced flyer may wait for several days for winds to gather strength so it can rise aloft.

Even for experienced older birds, takeoff is an awkward process. Albatrosses rely on fast winds in which they can glide, swoop, and soar with ease. This is partly why they range across the lower parts of the globe, just north of the Antarctic. There, regular strong winds blow in areas called the roaring forties and howling fifties.

Lonely life

For most species of albatross, breeding time begins in spring. The male and female, who are a lifelong mated pair, rattle and clack their beaks to each other as they court. They also make groaning and snoring noises, and dance awkwardly in front of each other, holding out their wings.

The pair make a cup-shaped nest of mud, earth, and bits of plants, such as grass stems and roots. Or they may repair an old nest from a previous year. The single egg is kept warm and protected by each parent in turn. It does not hatch until 65 to 80 days later, one of the longest incubation periods of any bird.

The new chick is fluffy brown-gray at first. Then it grows a warm coat of downy, whiter feathers. The

BABY FACTFILE

ANIMAL
Albatross, 14 species
SCIENTIFIC NAME
Bird family Diomedeidae
DISTRIBUTION
Mainly southern oceans, but wanders over all oceans
SIZE OF MOTHER
Length 3-4 feet from beak to tail; wingspan 9 feet or more
LENGTH OF INCUBATION
9-12 weeks
NUMBER OF BABIES
1 egg
SIZE AT BIRTH
Length about 10-16 inches
EARLY DEVELOPMENT
In most species, the chick is guarded and fed by parents in turn; later it is left alone for long periods as both parents fly off to gather food
WHEN INDEPENDENT
Flies at 4-9 months; parents continue to feed chick for up to one year
WHEN ABLE TO BREED
About 5 years, but many albatrosses do not breed until 10 years or older

Above *An albatross settles itself down into its nest mound, for its turn at incubation.*

Opposite *The straggly, downy plumage of this Laysan albatross chick will gradually be replaced by smooth flight feathers.*

Right *This immature albatross stretches its immense wings as it prepares for its first flight from the Midway Atoll in the Pacific Ocean.*

parents take turns to stay with it for the first few weeks. One keeps the baby warm and protected, while the other flies away to feed for a few days. The absent parent returns with a stomach full of half-digested food, such as squid, fish, and shellfish which it regurgitates.

Should an animal or human intruder approach, the parent sits on the nest and snaps its bill angrily. If this fails, it spits out some of the vile-smelling, oily fluid from its stomach. After several weeks, both parents go off to feed and the chick is left alone. If it is in danger, it spits vile-smelling oil at the attacker. Every week or two, one parent brings a large meal of semidigested fish for the baby. The chick may wander around the breeding areas while the parents are away, but it runs back to the nest when one returns.

The parents feed their chick in this pattern for up to one year. This means the youngster has to endure the howling winter gales and rain mainly on its own. It also means, for the larger albatross species that the whole time period of courting, mating, incubating the egg, and feeding the youngster takes more than one year. So bigger albatrosses can breed only once every two or even three years.

The young albatross makes its first flight about four to nine months after hatching. It gradually learns to swoop over the sea's surface and catch fish and squid, which it will do for its lifespan of 30 years or more.

LEATHERBACK TURTLE

*Newly hatched baby turtles must run the
gauntlet of many predators, from gulls to
foxes, as they race to the sea.*

The leatherback is the biggest of the world's seven kinds of sea turtles. A very large, old individual may have a shell longer than 7 feet. Its enormous front flippers, stretched out sideways, measure 9 feet from tip to tip.

Newly hatched leatherback turtles would fit in the palm of your hand. They are miniature versions of their parents except for a small difference in coloration. Adult turtles are mainly dark brown but can also be almost black. The babies have white or pale yellow spots along their neck and flipper edges.

Above *Having bitten their way out of their shells, the baby leatherbacks must struggle and "swim" up from their sandy pit to reach the surface.*

BABY FACTFILE

ANIMAL
Leatherback turtle, leathery turtle

SCIENTIFIC NAME
Dermochelys coriacea

DISTRIBUTION
World seas from North America, Scandinavia, and Japan down to the tip of South America, Africa, and Australia; mainly in warmer waters

SIZE OF MOTHER
Length of shell up to 7 feet; weight over 1,000 pounds

LENGTH OF INCUBATION
7 weeks

NUMBER OF EGGS
60-100 per clutch, up to 9 clutches per season

SIZE AT BIRTH
Length about 2½ inches

EARLY DEVELOPMENT
Scales on skin disappear after 2 months

WHEN INDEPENDENT
At hatching

WHEN ABLE TO BREED
5-10 years

Under cover of darkness, the mother leatherback turtle hauls herself ashore onto the breeding beach. Sometimes a group of females arrives on the same night. When each reaches dry sand above the tideline, she digs a pit with all four flippers. Then she lays about 60 to 100 pale-shelled eggs, refills the pit with sand, and circles the site for up to an hour. Finally and laboriously, she drags herself back to the sea. She will never see her babies. And she repeats this process several times each breeding season.

Seven weeks later, the babies hatch on the sandy beach. From that moment on, each young turtle is at the mercy of three types of predators. First, there are the land-based predators, ranging from lizards to raccoons and rats. From the air, gulls, skuas, and other seabirds pose a constant threat. When the baby reaches the sea, fish and squid are the chief dangers.

Jellyfish meals

The newly hatched baby leatherbacks first run the gauntlet of the beach. Then they splash into the shallows to test the swimming power of their front flippers. The leatherback is the strongest swimmer among sea turtles and ranges for thousands of miles across the open oceans. Leatherbacks also dive deep, though like any reptile, they breathe air and must surface regularly for a fresh breath. They may stray far from their preferred tropical waters, into the cooler seas farther north and south.

If the youngster survives the many early hazards, it learns to catch and chop up its favorite food of jellyfish, using its sharp-edged, horny mouth. It also feeds on other soft-bodied floating creatures. The usual turtle shell's bony plates are covered with a leathery skin which gives this creature its name.

Like the other sea turtles, leatherbacks face dangers from people. Turtle eggs are dug up and eaten. Breeding beaches are discovered by tourists. Then, when the mother turtle returns to breed, she is disturbed by bright lights, noises, and traffic.

Above Race for life – newly hatched turtles rush for the sea to escape the gulls, foxes, and other predators that come to feast on them.

Left Photographed at night with the aid of special lighting, this leatherback female has begun to lay her eggs in a pit she has dug in the sand.

SEA OTTER

Sea otters are fully adapted for their life in the sea and rarely come onto dry land – except, perhaps, to give birth.

Of the 12 kinds, or species, of otters around the world, the sea otter is the one most adapted to life in the water. Its glossy, dense fur keeps its body dry and warm even in cold seas. The otter cleans and grooms the fur almost constantly so that it stays waterproof and retains warmth.

The sea otter's front paws have very small toes and look more like mittens than paws. Its back feet are large and flipperlike for powerful swimming. The sea otter spends almost all of its life in the water, occasionally coming ashore to give birth.

Well-developed baby

The female has a single baby, rarely twins, up to nine months after mating. This long pregnancy period is due partly to delayed implantation (see "American Badger" on pages 134 to 135). The long pregnancy also allows the baby otter to reach a well-developed stage inside the womb. At birth it is fully furred, has a complete set of milk (or first teeth) and its eyes are open and alert.

The otter baby, or pup, may be born on the shore, though some are born in the water. This is one of the few times it will be on land, and it does not stay there for long. Almost at once, the mother carries the newborn by the scruff of its neck to the water. She

BABY FACTFILE

ANIMAL
Sea otter

SCIENTIFIC NAME
Enhydra lutris

DISTRIBUTION
Rocky coasts of Bering Sea, Pacific coasts of Asia and North America down to California

SIZE OF MOTHER
Length of head and body 3-4 feet, tail 10-14 inches; weight 60-90 pounds

LENGTH OF PREGNANCY
8-9 weeks

NUMBER OF BABIES
1 pup every other year

SIZE AT BIRTH
Length 8-12 inches

EARLY DEVELOPMENT
Born well developed with full set of milk teeth, fur, and eyes open

WHEN INDEPENDENT
About 8 months

WHEN ABLE TO BREED
4 years or more

Left *Heads or tails? A young sea otter curls up, its thick fur fluffily dry.*

Right *In this typical scene, the sea otter mother floats lazily on her back and naps, while the young pup looks around with interest.*

Right *The classic sea otter baby pose – a tiny, furry bundle asleep on mother's chest.*

Opposite *Parent and youngster look alert as they "sit up" and peer over the waves to survey the seascape. Their furry whiskers help them to feel their way underwater.*

rolls over and swims on her back, and the pup lies on her stomach. There it can feed on her milk, and the mother can clean and groom her offspring.

The new pup's fur is fawn, a lighter color than the adult's dark brown body and straw-colored head. Also, its tail is untapered, and rather short and flat compared with the adult's.

Diving for food

Sea otters rarely swim in the open ocean. They spend most of their lives in shallow water, usually less than 100 feet deep, within a mile of the shore. There they dive to catch bottom-living shellfish such as abalone, clams, and mussels. They also prey on crabs, sea snails, sea urchins, and fish.

The female otter teaches her youngster how to catch food and how to handle it when eating. One common method is to dive down to the seabed, and dig in the mud and pebbles for clams and other shellfish. The otter closes its ears and nostrils for the dive. Since the water is often murky, it depends on its sensitive hands and well-whiskered muzzle to find prey. It may take two or three dives, each lasting up to a minute, to dig out a food item. Alternatively, the otter may grab a small rock and chip an abalone from the underwater rocks.

Sea otters are renowned for their use of rocks as tools. Apart from primates such as humans and apes, they are one of the few animals that use tools.

After diving, the sea otter returns to the surface with its catch between its paws. Usually it has a small, smooth, flat rock, too. The otter floats on the surface, rolls on its back, and uses its belly as a dining table. It places the stone on its stomach and bangs the shellfish against it until the shell cracks. It may take more than 20 blows, at two per second, before the otter can bite and lick out the flesh inside.

The young otter follows its mother on dives. Its basic food-catching behavior is instinctive, but it must have plenty of practice before it can gather enough to eat. A sea otter uses lots of energy in keeping warm, so it needs to consume about one-quarter of its body weight daily. For several weeks, the mother shares her food with her youngster.

Sea otters even sleep on the ocean. They wind themselves into the floating fronds of kelp and other seaweeds. The weeds help to reduce the size of incoming waves from the open ocean. They also stop the dozing otters from drifting out to sea. In addition, the kelp beds hamper the activities of the sea otter's main predators – killer whales and hunting fish such as sharks.

GANNET

The noise in a gannet colony is deafening, as up to 50,000 birds squawk and fence with their bills.

Gannets are goose-sized, gull-like seabirds related to pelicans and cormorants. They have long, sharp, dartlike beaks and spend much of their lives at sea. There they plunge like arrows into the water, from heights of 100 feet or more, after fish, squid, and other sea creatures.

These birds congregate in the thousands, in breeding colonies on cliffs, steep ledges, and rocky outcrops. The breeding colonies are located on isolated islands that few predators can reach. The baby gannet hatches into a bustling world of crashing waves, and the comings and goings of thousands of parents. Each nest is an untidy pile of seaweeds, grasses, earth, and other materials, glued with droppings.

The male gannets arrive at the colony first and fight for last year's nesting sites. Then the females appear, and the birds pair up, usually for life. Gannet courtship displays are lengthy and comical, yet touching. The partners grasp each other's sharp beaks, push and pull, hold each other's head or neck by the beak, grapple and wrestle, and peck each other. They also wave their beaks to the sky and carry out other elaborate movements. These noisy displays continue through the breeding season.

Above *Its down ruffling in the wind, this gannet chick waits for its parent to return to the nest with a meal.*

Below *Which one's yours? Neighboring gannets are typically just out of beak reach in their colony on Bird Island, South Africa.*

BABY FACTFILE

ANIMAL
Gannet, common gannet

SCIENTIFIC NAME
Sula (Morus) bassana

DISTRIBUTION
Spends most of its time at sea but breeds on coasts around northern Atlantic Ocean

SIZE OF MOTHER
Length beak to tail 34-40 inches; weight up to 8 pounds

LENGTH OF INCUBATION
6-7 weeks

NUMBER OF BABIES
1 egg

SIZE AT BIRTH
Length of egg 3 inches, chick 4-6 inches

EARLY DEVELOPMENT
New chick soon grows thin down, opens its eyes at 3 days, feeds hungrily at any time; by 11 weeks weighs more than parent

WHEN INDEPENDENT
10-12 weeks, flies at 13-15 weeks

WHEN ABLE TO BREED
4-5 years

Left *A gannet chick greedily gobbles down the half-digested food brought back by its parent. Various types of birds regurgitate food in this manner for their offspring.*

Territory disputes sometimes break out between nesting neighbors. The nests are only 2 to 3 feet apart, just out of reach of next-door's beak. Each pair of birds guards their nest and the small area around with great vigor, and attacks any intruders.

Several weeks after courtship begins, in early summer, the female lays a single bluish egg. This slowly turns white, then becomes stained with nest materials and droppings. Each parent takes a turn protecting the egg for one or two days, holding it between webbed feet, while the mate dives for fish.

Huge appetite

The chick takes up to a day to peck through the thick eggshell. It is naked, but soon grows a thin coat of down feathers and opens its eyes after about three days. The baby sits on a parent's feet, then sits in the nest while the parents find food.

The chick lives up to the saying "as greedy as a gannet." When a parent returns from a fishing trip, the baby eagerly thrusts its head down the adult's throat and gobbles up the part-digested fish and other contents of the parent's crop (storage stomach). The greedy youngster grows very fast. Its fluffy feathers, which make it look enormous, are gradually replaced by adult feathers. The youngster's feathers are speckled brown, while the adults are pure white.

By the age of 11 weeks, the chick weighs a quarter more than as its parent! At this age, the parents abandon their chick, and hunger forces it to leave the nest. Too heavy to fly, it rushes through the colony toward the water, risking pecks and injury from other gannets. Once at sea, the youngster paddles and dives to catch mackerel, herring, and other fish.

A few weeks later, the chick can take to the air. In their first few years, many young gannets migrate to the coast of west Africa. Older birds stay nearer to the nest site, ready for the next busy breeding season.

WHALES AND DOLPHINS

The world's biggest animal baby is the blue whale calf. It is longer than a family automobile and drinks 80 gallons of milk daily!

As a group, whales and dolphins, including porpoises, are known as cetaceans. There are 76 kinds, or species, of cetaceans spread around all of the world's oceans and in some major rivers, too.

The whale's distant ancestors once lived on land, but then they returned to the water. During millions of years of evolution, the whale's front legs became flippers and its back legs disappeared. Large horizontal flukes, the "tail," developed at the rear of

BABY FACTFILE

ANIMAL
Whales and dolphins

SCIENTIFIC NAME
Mammal order Cetacea

DISTRIBUTION
All of the world's oceans; river dolphins in major rivers of Asia and South America

SIZE OF MOTHER
Length from 4 feet in smallest dolphins to over 90 feet in biggest whales

LENGTH OF PREGNANCY
About 9 months in smaller dolphins to 18 months in beaked whales

NUMBER OF BABIES
Usually 1 calf

SIZE AT BIRTH
Length 1-2 feet for small dolphins to 25 feet for blue whale calf

EARLY DEVELOPMENT
Newborn looks like small adult; can swim, dive, and feed within minutes of birth

WHEN INDEPENDENT
At 6-8 months in smaller species, up to 2 years in larger ones

WHEN ABLE TO BREED
From about 5 years in small species to over 20 years in large species

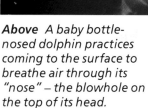

Above *A baby bottle-nosed dolphin practices coming to the surface to breathe air through its "nose" – the blowhole on the top of its head.*

Right *The world's largest baby, a leaping blue whale calf, attempts "breaching." Swimming horizontally at maximum speed, the whale propels itself almost clear of the water, vaults, and falls back with a gigantic splash.*

the body. The whale is now the most completely aquatic of all the mammals.

Blue whale

The largest animal in the world today is the blue whale (*Balaenoptera musculus*). Specimens have measured about 100 feet long and over 150 tons. The world's biggest animal has the world's biggest baby. A newborn blue whale, called a calf, is almost 25 feet long and weighs up to 3 tons.

The calf is born in the usual mammal way, since whales are mammals not fish. The baby slips from the birth opening and the mother nudges it to the surface so that it can take its first breaths of air. It breathes through its blowhole, which is the nasal opening or nostrils on the top of its head.

Fastest growth

Like all mammals, the blue whale female feeds her calf on milk. The baby takes in a lot of milk – about 80 gallons each day! The milk is thick and amazingly rich, especially in calcium and phosphorus. These are used by the calf to build up a thick layer of fatty blubber under the skin, to keep in its body warmth.

The calf grows at an astonishing rate. It puts on 200 pounds daily at first. By the time it is weaned, at about seven months, it has almost doubled its birth length.

After weaning, the blue whale calf eats the same food as the adults, mainly krill. These are finger-sized crustaceans that resemble shrimp. The whale opens its vast mouth, takes a great gulp of water, and closes its mouth again. Using its chin, cheek, and tongue, the whale squeezes the water out through fringed strips, known as baleen plates, in the mouth. The baleen plates hang from its jaws like large combs and filter food items from the water. The whale then licks off the food and swallows it.

During the summer, the blue whales feed in the polar waters of the far north and south, each eating about four tons a day. In the fall, the whales migrate back to warmer tropical waters. Then the females, which mated 10 to 12 months earlier, give birth to their calves.

Gray whales

The gray whale (*Eschrichtius robustus*) is familiar to many people living on the Pacific coast of North America. Gray whales tend to live and travel near the coast, and they can be observed from boats or the shore. They spend the summer feeding in the far north, off Alaska. In the fall, they migrate to breed in southern waters, especially off Baja California. There the calves are born in the warm shallows.

The gray whale calf is about 16 feet long at birth and looks much sleeker than the lumpy, barnacle-

Right The sperm whale is the largest true carnivore on Earth. A formidable predator, it may reach up to 60 feet long. It preys upon big fish, giant squid, and octopus. This is a mother with her two-day-old calf, which is already 14 feet in length.

Above *Among toothed whales, the orca, or killer whale, is the largest member of the dolphin family. Eight feet long at birth, this young calf may grow to 30 feet as an adult. Intelligent and fearless, a pod of orcas will hunt cooperatively, encircling and attacking blue whales.*

encrusted adult. The newborn calf does not have an insulating layer of blubber under its skin. This starts to build up over the two months that the whales stay in their warm lagoons. The body blubber continues to thicken while the mother and baby swim north. By the time they reach the Arctic summer feeding areas, the calf is fully protected against the cold water.

Dolphins

Bottle-nosed dolphins (*Tursiops truncatus*) are found in the coastal waters of most seas. They live in groups of 10 to 20, and feed mainly on bottom-dwelling fish and squid. A pair of courting dolphins swim with and caress each other. The female is pregnant for one year, and then the baby is born tail first. Two female "midwife" dolphins stay close by during the birth, and they help the calf to the surface for its first breaths.

The baby bottle-nosed dolphin feeds on its mother's milk for about one year. Since the pregnancy also lasts this long, the adult females can have a baby only once every two or three years. The interval between breeding is even longer in whales. This is one reason why whale populations, devastated by the whaling industry, will take many years to recover. Some of these slow breeders may never regain their former numbers.

INDEX

*Figures in italic indicate
photographs.*

ACKNOWLEDGMENTS

Quarto Publishing plc would like to thank the following for providing photographs and for permission to reproduce copyrighted material:

Alan and Sandy Carey – pages 2, 123, 135, 165, and back jacket; Francois Gohier – page 171.

All other photographs supplied by Bruce Coleman Ltd.

The publishers would like to thank Dr. Gary San Julian, Ms. Carol Boggis, Ms. Susan Bond, and Ms. Susan Oesch of the National Wildlife Federation for their time, knowledge, and talents in reviewing the manuscript.